The Coach's Survival Guide

The Coach's Survival Guide

Kim Morgan

 Open University Press

Open University Press
McGraw-Hill Education
8th Floor, 338 Euston Road
London
NW1 3BH

and Two Penn Plaza, New York, NY 10121-2289, USA

First published 2019

Senior Commissioning Editor: Hannah Kenner
Editorial Assistant: Karen Harris
Content Product Manager: Ali Davis

A catalogue record of this book is available from the British Library

ISBN-13: 9780335227020
ISBN-10: 0335227023
eISBN: 9780335227037

Library of Congress Cataloging-in-Publication Data
CIP data applied for

Typeset by Transforma Pvt. Ltd., Chennai, India

Printed and bound by CPI Group (UK) Ltd, Croydon, CR0 4YY

Praise for this book

"This book is an act of generosity towards coaches and ultimately towards coachees. No coach needs to be alone with the problems and dilemmas that inherently exist in our practice. Kim has a warm smile and a practical stance that lets wisdom and empowerment leap off the page."

Claire Genkai Breeze, Relume Challenger Spirit

"Kim Morgan possesses a unique brand of humility, humour and hard-won experience which she shares with us in her customary generous and fascinating style. Reading this book was like spending time with a close friend; a combination of warmth, wit and illumination."

Professor Damian Hughes, Professor of Organisational
Psychology and Change

"This book is an essential companion to anyone setting out as a professional coach. It provides knowledge, expertise and, perhaps most importantly, comfort for all the challenges that new coaches face. Carry it around with you at all times!"

Tom Preston. C.E.O. The Preston Associates

"The art of powerful writing comes when an author writes 'what they know' and with the Coach's Survival Guide, Kim is clearly on home territory. Whilst coming from a base of thorough study and research, the guidance here is practical, wise and ultimately accessible. Storytelling explains key principles in a way that mere theory cannot, and I particularly enjoyed the case studies and recognised the truth telling within. Congratulations Kim, another valuable addition to the profession."

Julie Starr, author of The Coaching Manual

"This is a hugely practical and accessible support guide to help you address the challenges you will face in developing your coaching practice, from setting up your practice, generating clients and managing yourself in the coaching relationship.

Kim has reached these critical practitioner insights through lengthy trial and error to help you avoid the many professional pitfalls you will inevitably encounter and, therefore, save you time, money and energy."

John Leary-Joyce, Exec Chair AoEC International,
author Fertile Void

Contents

List of Case Studies   ix
List of Figures   xi
List of Tables   xii

Introduction   1

Normalizing the insecurities felt by many coaches; acknowledging the realities of building a coaching business and addressing the everyday issues that can hinder a coach's performance; setting out the approach of this book – a survival guide to help you thrive.

1. Credibility   4

Building credibility as a new coach; what qualifications and accreditations do clients look for? How choosing a niche or specialism can help you to get seen and heard; some guidelines for a successful chemistry session; coaching exercises to increase your credibility and assess your sphere of influence.

2. Building a Coaching Business   17

Applying the principles of coaching to building a successful coaching business; marketing your business and setting your fees; why business plans are so important and some tips on planning for growth; coaching exercises to identify your strengths as an entrepreneur.

3. Overcoming Impostor Syndrome   29

The links between Impostor Syndrome and starting a new career; building confidence and competence when you feel like a fraud; how to know if you are doing a good job; the unexpected benefits of being a novice coach; coaching exercises for dealing with Impostor Syndrome.

4. Contracting, Pitching and Client Meetings   42

Why contracting matters and how to formally contract with different clients; three-way meetings with clients in organizations; how to pitch your services in meetings, presentations and panel interviews; coaching exercises to help you prepare for selling your services.

5. Managing Client Boundaries   **54**

*How much should I disclose about myself and my own life to my clients?
What do I do if my client cries? What if I don't like my client? Are you ever
'off-duty' as a coach?*

6. Boundaries of Time and Place   **66**

*Where should coaching sessions take place? The pros and cons of various
locations; creating a 'safe container' for your client; managing your time
boundaries; the door handle moment in coaching.*

7. Facilitating Change   **79**

*Understanding how change happens; measuring the client's readiness
for change; using change models; the role of the coach; does all
coaching have to be transformative?*

8. Group Coaching   **94**

*The differences between group and team coaching; skills and experience
required to coach more than one person; maintaining a coaching stance
when coaching a group; working with a co-coach; benefits of group
coaching; reflection exercises for group coaching.*

9. Coaching Dilemmas   **107**

*What do I do if my client is resistant to being coached? How much should
I chase a client who cancels appointments? What if my client is
already seeing another coach or therapist? Who is my client – the
organization or the coachee?*

10. When Will I Know Enough?   **124**

*How, where and when to use the techniques from your coaching toolkit;
the primacy of the coaching relationship; do you need further training?
A reflection exercise to establish your preferences and default
coaching style.*

11. Self-Care for Coaches   **136**

*The benefits of practising self-care and its impact on your coaching;
some practical suggestions for physical, emotional, spiritual, social,
psychological, financial and professional self-care; why coaching
supervision is so important; building a 'self-care plan'.*

Conclusion and Closing Comments   **149**

References   151
Index   157

List of Case Studies

Case Study 1.1: Simon   6

Case Study 1.2: Doreen   8

Case Study 1.3: Sacha   11

Case Study 1.4: Carly   12

Case Study 2.1: Luke   19

Case Study 2.2: Josephine   20

Case Study 2.3: Amanda   23

Case Study 2.4: Antonio   25

Case Study 3.1: Lauren   29

Case Study 3.2: Suzy   31

Case Study 3.3: Alison   33

Case Study 3.4: Dave   36

Case Study 4.1: Alice   43

Case Study 4.2: Hope   46

Case Study 4.3: Hayley   48

Case Study 4.4: Christine   49

Case Study 5.1: Rachel   55

Case Study 5.2: Babs   58

Case Study 5.3: John and Sandra   60

Case Study 5.4: Bob   61

Case Study 6.1: Chris   67

Case Study 6.2: Toni   68

Case Study 6.3: Owen   72

Case Study 6.4: Kiran   73

Case Study 6.5: Anna   74

Case Study 7.1: Betty   80

Case Study 7.2: Amy   82

Case Study 7.3: George   85

Case Study 7.4: Jo   87

Case Study 8.1: Teresa   96

Case Study 8.2: Tom   97

Case Study 8.3: Cara   102

Case Study 8.4: Ella   103

Case Study 9.1: Sarah   107

Case Study 9.2: Peter   108

Case Study 9.3: Colin   112

Case Study 9.4: Jason   115

Case Study 9.5: Valentina   116
Case Study 9.6: Derek   117
Case Study 9.7: Stella   121
Case Study 10.1: Melissa   125
Case Study 10.2: Brian   127
Case Study 11.1: Sushma   137
Case Study 11.2: Diana   139
Case Study 11.3: Sam   143

List of Figures

Figure 2.1   Wheel of business focus   26
Figure 2.2   Wheel of entrepreneurial traits   27

List of Tables

Table 1.1   Coach credibility appraisal   15
Table 2.1   Price rise indicators   22
Table 3.1   Write your own reference   41
Table 8.1   Prerequisites for group or team coaching   106

Introduction

Welcome to *The Coach's Survival Guide*.

The idea for this book developed from my twenty years' experience of delivering coach training programmes and having also provided coaching supervision and continuing professional development (CPD) to thousands of coaches. Over this time both newly trained and experienced coaches have brought recurring issues to supervision sessions or contacted me with the same repeating dilemmas and questions about their coaching practice. When I decided to write this book, it was because I found myself answering the same questions once again with a new group of coaches. Over time I had also noticed the same questions regularly appearing on online coaching forums, posed by coaches around the world. That made me realize that it wasn't just the coaches I heard from who still had unanswered questions, but it was common to most new coaches.

Here are just some of the frequently asked questions:

- How do I stop my coaching sessions running over time?
- I feel intimidated by successful clients. Should I stop coaching them?
- Do I need to get more qualifications or is my coaching qualification enough?
- Do I need a niche for my business?
- Can I do group or team coaching now I have trained as a coach?
- How do I conduct a successful triad meeting or chemistry session?
- Where should I meet my clients for coaching?
- How do I deal with limiting beliefs – my own and my clients'?
- How do I establish credibility as a new coach?
- What if I don't like my client?
- How do I look after myself as a coach and a business owner?

Most coaches struggle with issues like these at some point. *The Coach's Survival Guide* seeks to normalize the almost inevitable feelings of self-doubt felt by coaches, particularly in the initial stages of their new career.

It is challenging enough to learn a whole new skillset, complete your academic and/or professional qualifications and immerse yourself in the processes, ethics and guidelines of a new industry, without also entering the world of self-employment for the first time. On top of all this, you may be returning to work after a career break, have left a job you have had for a long time or been through a redundancy process. You may have invested a lot of money in retraining and be under pressure to generate income quickly from your new career. It is no wonder that new coaches have lots of questions, because there are so many new skills and so much information to assimilate quickly. To add to the uncertainty, because there is no overarching regulatory body for coaching, the answer to a lot of coaching dilemmas is often 'It depends'. This is not always what you want to hear when you are trying hard to get things 'right' as a new coach.

This book provides you with practical, instant support on the issues which are likely to crop up in your coaching work. It is not intended to replace formal coaching supervision, CPD or having your own coach, but rather as a first aid kit for those moments when you feel unsure about what to do or when you encounter a situation for the first time.

The book is aimed primarily at new coaches working in a freelance or self-employed role, but it is also intended to be a valuable resource for anyone involved in coaching, including trainers of coaches. If you are working as an internal coach in an organization and you have a longer-term plan to become a freelance coach, this book could give you valuable insight and preparation for what is to come.

- It is an easy to use, accessible, non-academic text. The book is firmly grounded in practice and experience.
- It includes case studies, drawn from real-life practice, although in all cases I have changed names, places and other identifying details to produce fictionalized versions of the case studies and protect the anonymity of individuals.
- The book also includes coaching exercises which you can use to reflect on your practice or which you can add to your coaching toolkit to use with clients.

If you want to dig deeper into any of the topics covered, further reading is suggested at the end of each chapter.

This book is rooted in the real world, normalizing the insecurities felt by many coaches, acknowledging the realities of building a coaching business and addressing the everyday issues that can hinder a coach's performance or confidence.

I have written the book to help you when you have left the safety of your coach training programme or your organization. This is the time when you find yourself discovering all the things you didn't know you needed to know about coaching. Although the book is not a coach training manual, it is likely that some of the topics covered in the book were covered on your coach training programme. If this is the case, perhaps you will be familiar with some of the information. On the other hand, they may be some of the pieces of information which passed you by, or which didn't seem relevant at the time, but they have suddenly become relevant. Designed for everyday use, this book is a resource that will accompany you on your journey from novice to experienced coach.

How to Use the Book

Each chapter stands alone and does not need to be read in conjunction with the other chapters, or even in sequence. There are occasional cross-references to other chapters, but mostly only to highlight that there is further discussion about a topic in another chapter. The book, as its title suggests, is intended to be a survival guide – therefore it is a book to keep close at hand so that you can access instant support for any dilemmas which occur for you in your coaching practice.

Each chapter covers one topic from a number of different angles. The chapters cover issues such as: dealing with 'Impostor Syndrome' feelings, establishing credibility as a coach, knowing which technique to choose, working with limiting beliefs, boundaries, contracting and other meetings, issues and dilemmas about clients, coaching teams or groups, being self-employed and practising self-care.

There are case studies in each chapter, drawn from real-life experiences. The case studies can be used on coach training programmes for group discussions or by individuals to reflect on the question 'What would I do in this situation?' All the coaching exercises in the book are designed either for your own use or for you to use with your clients.

Throughout the book, you will notice that sometimes the person receiving coaching is referred to as the 'client' and other times as the 'coachee'. Usually the term 'coachee' is used to describe someone receiving coaching in an organizational context, and 'client' refers to a private coaching assignment.

The Approach

It is a challenge to maintain a coaching stance when setting out to write a book which provides answers to questions. Coaches usually ask the questions, rather than answering them. However, I have incorporated a coaching approach wherever possible, by presenting you with stories, information and options and encouraging you to develop the solutions which are right for you.

I have also taken a coaching approach in focusing on you and the part you play in your dilemma, rather than giving you a direct solution to it. I have assumed prior knowledge about the basics of coaching, and because every reader of this book will have different levels of knowledge and experience, for some people I will have assumed that you have too little knowledge and for others, too much. The book is jam-packed with information and ideas, so I hope that you find something of value in it for you. Each of the chapters could be a book in its own right and, indeed, there are existing books which are devoted to the individual chapter topics in this guide. That means that in this book I have prioritized breadth rather than depth, but I hope nevertheless to have distilled deep knowledge and experience into fewer words and lots of topics.

I hope the book helps you not only to survive, but to thrive in the world of coaching.

1 Credibility

Organizations frequently approach me to coach a leader who is technically skilled, but lacks credibility, presence and gravitas. These three words are often grouped together, but when I ask organizations to define them, they are at a loss to do so. Credibility seems to be a universal intangible, yet organizations, and individual clients, expect coaches to exhibit it. This chapter will attempt to determine what it looks, sounds and feels like to possess credibility, presence and gravitas. It will also look at various approaches to overcoming the credibility trap and enhancing your credibility as a newly qualified coach.

Proving your Credentials

However confident you are in your ability as a coach, you may still have to prove your credibility to buyers of coaching. A lot of newly qualified coaches ask the question, 'Why would anyone find me credible as a coach when I haven't had any paying clients, don't have client testimonials and have obviously not been coaching for very long? I feel confident that I can do the job, but how can I get a foot in the door of an organization to prove myself without a track record?' This is a reasonable question. Organizations and individuals will often want to know the extent of your experience before engaging you as a coach. This can leave new coaches feeling that they are stuck in a 'chicken and egg' situation.

Organizations appointing external coaches normally require them to have a recognized professional coaching qualification, to be under regular coaching supervision and to be engaged in continuous professional development. They may also require them to be members of a recognized professional coaching body. In the 2016 International Coach Federation (ICF) Global Coaching Survey (ICF 2016: 27), 77 per cent of coach practitioners agreed that individual clients and organizations expect their coaches to be professionally accredited.

The *6th Ridler Report* (Mann 2016: 59) showed that 68 per cent of organizations look for external coaches with accreditation from a professional body, and that organizations generally have an expectation that external coaches will have a higher level of qualification than the organization's internally trained coaches.

These organizations considered a professional coaching accreditation to be a necessary indicator of coaching capability, but not sufficient by itself. They typically wanted more evidence of the coach's suitability to work with them. Organizations and individual clients often look for coaches who have had professional experience of their industry or sector.

Many people looking for a coach do not understand exactly how coaching works and therefore assume that the coach they are looking for needs knowledge or experience of their work context. Some believe that a coach needs to have achieved the same level of seniority in their own previous career as the person they are coaching. Clients often ask for a coach who can match their own work experience. So a CEO will request a coach who has been a CEO and a teacher will look for a coach who has worked in education. But in fact, while having experience of your client's work context is helpful if you are mentoring them, it can actually be a hindrance in coaching. You may be called on to play the role of expert in other aspects of your life, but when you are coaching, an 'expert' mindset will tend to limit your creativity and inhibit your curiosity. It can be more effective to approach the situation as a beginner. When you coach in a familiar context, you may be tempted to offer advice. When you have no experience of the client's world, you will be unable to recommend solutions and only be able to ask questions from a position of curiosity and not-knowing, which will allow the client to find the answers that work for them. We see similar ideas in the following quotation:

> If your mind is empty, it is always ready for anything; it is open to everything. In the beginner's mind there are many possibilities; in the expert's mind there are few.
>
> (Suzuki 1970: 2)

If you are wondering how to establish credibility in your new career, you may have also considered whether you should develop an area of expertise that would differentiate you from other coaches. For instance, you could perhaps establish your credibility as a subject matter expert, or specialize in coaching leaders, health professionals or people who need to build resilience or assertiveness. If you are considering offering coaching in a specific niche, it is likely that you will face the same challenge of having to demonstrate previous experience and success in this area.

There is also the issue of 'fit' and the fact that people like people who are like them. I remember once going for a coaching chemistry meeting at a television production company. As soon as I walked through the door, I knew that I was not going to get the work. It was a noisy open-plan office and everyone I saw was in their twenties, wearing jeans and t-shirts. Silence reigned as I teetered through the office in heels and a sober business suit, carrying a briefcase – I felt so corporate and 'old school' and I knew that I had completely misjudged how to present myself. I was battling against a complete sartorial mismatch before we had even started the chemistry meeting. The frustrating part of this was that I don't usually dress in such a formal way. I had been star-struck by the idea of working in television and made all kinds of incorrect assumptions about how I should present myself, and ended up looking like I was presenting the news.

Establishing Credibility as a Coach in New and Different Sectors

Case Study 1.1: Simon

Simon had worked as a senior manager in local government before retraining as a coach. He left local government because he was disillusioned and wanted to do something he considered to be more fulfilling and exciting. He was also looking for increased financial reward. Simon was aware of the high fees charged by some executive coaches. During his coach training programme, he decided that he would like to focus on coaching senior leaders in corporate organizations. He wanted to leave his local government background behind. He was looking for a change of career and a change of environment. Simon's plan was to work four days a week delivering only one-to-one executive coaching. But seven months after completing his coach training course and acquiring his coaching credentials and qualifications, Simon has yet to secure an executive coaching client. He has taken some coaching work in local government, which his previous employer offered him, and has delivered coaching in the voluntary sector, receiving great feedback from his clients and their organizations. He is confused about his inability to secure any work in the corporate sector and wonders what he needs to do to break into this market.

When people leave corporate roles to retrain as coaches, a few of them are fortunate enough to have negotiated some freelance coaching work as self-employed consultants with their previous employers. This eases their transition into self-employment and gives them peace of mind about a level of guaranteed work and income in the first months of their new career. It also usually means that they have accepted the fact that they already have credibility in their previous organization, and quite possibly within the wider industry sector. Therefore, they may decide to focus their future marketing efforts in the sector or industry where they are known and in which they do not have to prove their credibility. Other coaches take the same route of selling themselves back into the world they know and to people with whom they have existing relationships, even if they do not secure a freelance contract as part of their exit package with their previous employer.

Many newly trained coaches have retired or walked away from a senior corporate career and are financially independent. This type of coach is not usually working for the money but to give something back, have some work–life balance and find a sense of purpose. They are interested in undertaking coaching work that appeals to them and meets their values, rather than the fee associated with the work. They are sometimes keen to escape the world of business and are not looking to coach senior leaders, although it often turns out that they are in demand to do so because of the senior roles they have had and the perception that to coach a CEO you need to have been a CEO.

However, some new coaches are eager to leave their previous organization, sector or industry. They are looking not only for a change of career, but also a change of environment. Simon falls into this category. The problem for Simon is that he has never worked in the environment in which he wants to coach. Other new coaches who have been on a prolonged career break may have experience in the sectors in which they want to work, but none of it sufficiently recent or relevant.

In my experience, the coaches who transition most successfully into self-employment have proven credibility in the environment in which they are offering coaching. This makes life more difficult for coaches like Simon in Case Study 1.1 who want to coach in a new and different arena. If, like Simon, your previous career experience is not connected to the coaching you would like to begin to do, here are some options for enhancing your credibility in this new area.

Pro bono coaching experience

Many coach training organizations require you to undertake pro bono coaching with volunteer clients as part of your coach training programme or as part of the process to become an accredited coach. This is an opportunity for you to begin marketing yourself as a coach and to get some experience of working with your target clients. Simon, for example, could offer pro bono coaching sessions to senior leaders in the private corporate sector. In return, he could ask for a testimonial which he could use for marketing purposes and a referral to another volunteer client in the private sector. This would give Simon the opportunity to showcase his coaching skills and build some evidence of having coached senior leaders in the corporate sector. During the process, Simon would also discover whether he enjoyed working with this client group. I know many coaches who continue to offer pro bono coaching, alongside their paid work, if they are trying to break into a different market.

Establish yourself as a thought leader or subject matter expert

I can immediately think of people in my network who have successfully established themselves as the 'go-to' coaches for specific niche areas. These areas include coaching for specific contexts, such as the menopause, book writing, journaling, grief and loss, parenting, maternity leave, resilience, stress in the workplace and public speaking.

Case Study 1.2: Doreen

Doreen trained as a coach after a long and happy career in higher education. She planned to offer coaching in this sector and set out to offer a range of services, including one-to-one coaching for senior leaders in higher education; career coaching for graduates; training in coaching; and mentoring for staff and students. Doreen was confident that she had credibility and a wide network of contacts in higher education.

In her personal life Doreen had also been through a difficult divorce and had navigated her way through the online dating world for several years. She had eventually met and married the man of her dreams when she was in her late fifties. Doreen had become a bit of an 'expert' on recovering from a broken relationship and dating in later life. She talked with passion and enthusiasm about her experiences and people sought her out for support and guidance.

Before long, Doreen realized that, rather than finding a coaching niche for herself, the niche had found her. Previously she hadn't considered how her personal experiences could form part of her offer as a coach. She found that people wanted her help with their relationships and she discovered that she loved this work. Doreen gradually let her coaching work in education dwindle and she now works exclusively as a relationship coach.

There are many coaches, like Doreen in Case Study 1.2, who specialize in certain types of clients: professional musicians, creative artists, female CEOs, introverts or people who are looking for love. The measure of their success is that their name has become synonymous with the topic, which means that I and others automatically refer people to them if they are looking for a coach in this topic area. I am sure that there are other coaches working in these niche areas, but one of the things that distinguishes these coaches and identifies them as thought leaders is that they are driving some of the thinking and conversation about their chosen topic. They are innovating and contributing to the existing body of knowledge in their area. Some are published authors on their subject matter and others have delivered TEDx talks. These coaches are recognized as thought leaders by a wide range of people within and outside the coaching industry. Their status gives them the credibility to coach people of all levels of seniority and in different sectors and industries, allowing them to overcome the expectation that the coach will have experience in the client's sector.

If you are interested in achieving thought-leadership status, it requires significant dedication and commitment to developing your experience and knowledge of the subject. You will need to identify an area of genuine interest for you, ideally something in which you already have personal or professional experience. Consider what you are passionate about in life and in your work. Think about your values, your hobbies and interests, tasks that have given you pleasure, studies you have undertaken, charities you support and subjects on which you have strong, informed opinions. If you are already working as a coach, which clients do you feel most comfortable working with? Which clients have had the most value from working with you? If they have given you testimonials, what have they said about you? What kinds of clients create a feeling of confidence for you?

You are unlikely to become a thought leader on a topic in which you have no prior interest or experience and which does not reflect your life experiences. What elements of your own life story have been most significant, helpful, challenging or developmental for you? Remain aware that your life story will change over time and your ability to be an effective helper will be determined by your own circumstances and your ability to understand the needs of your clients. For example, the woman I know who specializes in menopause coaching only developed her niche offering after her own experience of the menopause and the difficulties it created for her in her role as a senior leader. When developing your ideas about thought leadership, it is also important for you to consider your credibility in coaching on your chosen topic. Would a premenopausal woman or a man be perceived as having credibility to coach women going through the menopause? Yes, of course it is possible, but they would need to be able to give evidence of some professional expertise about the subject in the absence of personal experience.

Be seen and heard

Having identified your area of thought leadership, your next step is to spread the word, raise your profile and ensure you reach as many people as possible with your message. In 1995, Harvey Coleman explored the value of exposure in achieving success. Coleman's research suggests that there are three elements we need to focus on if we are to achieve success and get to the top of the ladder: *performance*, meaning how good a job we do, what results we deliver; *image*, which is not merely how we are seen but how we are experienced by others, our personal 'brand'; and *exposure*, which involves ensuring that the right people know us, including those outside our own networks.

In his 1996 book (Coleman 1996: 21–3) *Empowering Yourself: The Organizational Game Revealed*, Coleman revealed some shocking statistics. His research suggests that performance counts for only 10 per cent of our success. Image contributes 30 per cent. Easily the largest component, at 60 per cent, is exposure.

Getting your message out to as many people as possible and raising your profile as a thought leader will mean writing regular articles and blogs on your specialist subject. You will need to think about getting your writing published in industry-specific publications as well as more mainstream magazines, journals or newspapers. If you manage to have something published on a website, blog or in a journal which has high credibility and high circulation, you will not only increase your reach but also benefit from an influential and high-quality affiliation. You will achieve credibility by proxy. Eventually you could work towards writing a book, which will propel you several rungs up the credibility ladder.

Do some public speaking to ensure that you are seen in person as well as in writing. Develop a compelling keynote presentation about your subject and contact companies, community groups, conference organizers, asking to be considered by them as a speaker at future events. You could even host your own event and invite influential friends and contacts to attend on the condition that they provide you with feedback and testimonials. Don't expect to be paid a speaker fee in the early stages of your speaking career. If you are not a confident public speaker and want to be seen as a thought leader, you will need to invest in some training in presentation skills.

Advertising and PR

Spreading your message to a roomful of people is cheaper and more effective than advertising as a way of raising your profile. Coaches often question whether to invest in advertising at all and there are people who will tell you that advertising doesn't work. I don't think it works as a one-off experiment, but regular and targeted advertising can help you build your brand and generate leads. Regular advertising requires financial investment. You will need to set a budget, start small and find out what works for you and reaches your target audience. Know what specific outcome you want to achieve from your advertising – for example, do you want people to book a free trial session with you? Use advertising to sponsor the things you are already doing, such as blogging, rather than seeing advertising as a separate activity for which you have to create new content.

If you have money to invest in your business, you could buy in some public relations (PR) support to fast-track your credibility as a thought leader. Like advertising, PR can be expensive, and you will need to allocate a budget and determine what return on investment would mean for you. A good PR company will find speaking and writing opportunities and create a media pack about you which may even lead to radio or television appearances. Journalists keep a list of people they can contact for an immediate response on specific topics when they crop up in the news and a PR company could ensure that you were on these lists for your area of expertise.

Be aware that promoting yourself will be time-consuming and potentially costly. Developing the skills to be an effective keynote speaker may require significant learning. It will probably take time to build your profile before your efforts and outlay are rewarded with income. You might get lucky and be snapped up on the speaker circuit, but usually it is a long game before fame comes knocking on your door.

Credibility by association

Most coaching companies use associate coaches when they need them on a freelance basis, so becoming an associate coach does not guarantee work. The coaching company will usually generate the clients and you will be contracted to deliver coaching on the company's behalf. Either there will be agreed associate fees, or the fees will be negotiated separately for each piece of work. The company will have a set of requirements and will put you through a selection process before accepting you as an associate coach. Requirements vary but are likely to include: professional and/or academic accreditation in coaching; membership of a professional coaching body; evidence of commitment to CPD and supervision; relevant professional insurance; references and testimonials; a certain number of years' experience of coaching. In some cases, coaching companies will also look for their associates to have significant leadership experience or psychological knowledge. Some may want associate coaches to be qualified in specific psychometric tests or diagnostics. If you are accepted as an associate coach, you will almost certainly be asked to sign an associate agreement with the coaching company. The agreement will set out the key terms of the agreement, the obligations of the associate coach role and invoicing and contracting arrangements.

Most associate coach roles are not exclusive, which means that you are usually free to register as an associate coach with more than one coaching company at any one time. Some coaching companies do ask for exclusivity. In this case, there may be additional selection criteria, which will include the expectation that you will generate clients for the coaching company and meet certain sales targets. The financial rewards are normally higher in this sort of arrangement, but the expectations on you are higher too.

The real benefit of being an associate coach is that you experience credibility by proxy from your association with a larger and more established coaching company. It is worth noting that at any one time there are more coaches looking for associate opportunities than there are coaching companies looking for associates. The eligibility criteria for becoming an associate coach can be demanding and some of the requirements may include significant previous coaching experience, which puts you back into the 'chicken and egg' credibility trap.

You may want to consider becoming a committee member on one of the professional coaching bodies. This will raise your profile and enhance your credibility by association. There may also be opportunities to write papers or blogs, run workshops or webinars or organize events, which would increase your exposure to more people in the coaching industry.

Case Study 1.3: Sacha

Sacha worked in the voluntary sector supporting adults with substance misuse issues. She had been considering doing a counselling qualification but decided on coach training instead. Sacha sailed through the training as most of it came easily to her, but she didn't feel she would ever be able to 'sell' herself as a coach because of her voluntary sector background. Other delegates on her coach training programme had business credibility, which Sacha felt she lacked.

When she finished her training, Sacha visited a counselling centre with one of her substance misuse clients and mentioned her coaching qualification in passing. To her delight, she was offered a position as 'The Counselling Centre Coach' for three days per week. She was the first coach to have been employed there. The counsellors had been considering incorporating a coach into their practice and Sacha was given the role because of her credibility in their eyes, which came from her experience of working with adults with complex needs.

Easy pickings

The safer and surer option is to begin working as a coach in the industry or environment with which you are familiar and in which you have existing contacts, respect, experience and credibility (Case Study 1.3). These are the easy pickings. It is important to build up a track record of coaching and to collect testimonials and referrals as you go. Let your professional and personal networks know about your new role as a coach and ask them to spread the word about you to their networks too. Spend some time perfecting your pitch about coaching and draw on your knowledge and experiences in your sector. People love to know that you understand what sorts of challenges they face on a daily basis in their working lives, and what coaching can do to support them with these challenges. Instead of resisting your previous experience, harness it to help you build your coaching business.

As you build your business, don't be lured, as Simon was, into imagining that you can earn telephone-number fees for your coaching when you have never charged those sorts of fees before. You need to build your reputation, your experience and your coaching hours before this can happen. Set realistic fees to reflect your level of expertise and experience, and get as much coaching experience as you can. When you find yourself with more clients than you can cope with, this will be a good signal that you are in higher demand and it will be time to increase your fees. As you coach more people, you will almost certainly start to receive referrals and requests from outside your usual environment, from different industries and from people with different levels of seniority.

Creating Chemistry

Case Study 1.4: Carly

Carly has a PhD and a string of other academic qualifications, along with an impressive CV and a strong coach profile. Carly qualified as a coach two years ago and decided that she did not want to start her own business, but to work as an associate coach for larger coaching companies. She knew that she would not be great at selling herself and thought that one way around that would be for an associate company to find the clients and win the coaching work, which she could then deliver on the associate company's behalf. Since registering as an associate coach, Carly has been put forward for a number of face-to-face 'chemistry' meetings or phone calls with clients. The clients usually speak to two or three coaches and then decide which coach they would like to work with. Carly is dismayed that she has never been selected, and wonders what she is doing or not doing to get this result every time. The associate company has not been able to give her any specific feedback. Carly suspects that she spends too much time talking about herself and her qualifications in a bid to establish her credibility. She would like to know how other coaches approach chemistry calls or chemistry meetings, but can't seem to get any specific answers.

In our organization, we put a lot of coaches forward for chemistry sessions with prospective clients. The idea of a chemistry session is for the client and the coach to determine in their own minds whether there is a good 'fit' between them in terms of interpersonal dynamics. It is an opportunity particularly for the client to assess whether the coach's style and approach will deliver the outcome they are looking for.

When we first started sending our associate coaches to participate in chemistry sessions, I expected that all of them would be chosen by different clients at different times because of the diverse range of characters and personality types involved in the process. To my surprise, this was not the case (see Case Study 1.4). I became aware quite soon that certain coaches are chosen time and time again by clients as the coach they would like to work with. This has led me to believe that mastering the challenge of a chemistry session is a skill in its own right and, like coaching, requires preparation, thought, attention and authenticity.

Guidelines for a successful chemistry session

Think in advance about how your client might be feeling and what they will need from the session. Give the client an opportunity to tell you their 'story' and to feel understood. Listen without judgement and with ease, not urgency. At this stage in the process, resist the temptation to bombard the client with clever coaching questions and to open up discussions that you cannot complete within the time frame of the chemistry session. Give the client a chance to ask you questions about how you might work together or about your previous experience of coaching. Tell stories of successful coaching outcomes and offer (anonymized) examples of how you have worked with other clients in similar situations or contexts. Ask questions about what the client wants and doesn't want from the coaching. It is useful to check the client's understanding of how coaching works and, if necessary, to reiterate that in coaching the client holds the agenda and needs to have a commitment to the coaching work. Demonstrate warmth, humour (if appropriate) and a lightness of touch.

It is particularly important to role model your way of working on boundaries and contracting in the chemistry session. State clearly how much time you have together for the session and ensure that you adhere to the time limit. Explain the limits of confidentiality surrounding the chemistry session. Be true to yourself and who you are as a coach. If the client says that they want a really pacy, challenging coach who will hold them to account and you know that you do not find it easy to work in this way, say so. You can also explain some of the alternative and equally effective techniques you employ to hold your clients to account.

I recently had a chemistry phone call with a client who insisted that they did not want to do any 'fluffy, psychological stuff' which was 'more like therapy than coaching'. As a coach with a background in psychotherapy, I knew that I would be inauthentic if I agreed to this. I explained that I don't believe that behaviour change can occur without belief change and that belief change does mean that we need to look at conditioning, values and repeating patterns in our behaviours. I also clarified that this does not need to be fluffy. I was true to myself, affirmed my way of working, and l let the client make a choice about whether to work with me based on honesty and clarity of communication.

Coaches who have a history of unsuccessful chemistry sessions have told me that they realize they have put too much emphasis on proving their credentials to the client and have forgotten about building rapport and using their coaching skills. They feel pressurized and put in the spotlight, which often triggers them to overperform. Coaches who have a history of successful chemistry sessions tell me that they set an intention to give the client a memorable experience of being coached. A chemistry session is not a sales pitch by the coach but a snapshot of coaching in action – an experience which offers support, challenge, listening, questioning and possibilities.

Coaching Exercises to Increase Credibility

What is it like to be coached by me?

This is a challenging exercise to do, but it can be useful in helping you understand your value and what personal and professional impact you bring to a coaching relationship. It can also highlight areas for development.

When I was a new coach, I once coached a client without discussing my fees in advance. Having coached him, he asked me how much he owed me, and I couldn't bring myself to ask for an appropriate fee. The client, who became frustrated with me, asked me to do this exercise. He invited me to change places with him and tell him what I thought it was like to be a client and to be coached by me. You might ask the question, 'Who was the coach here?' and you would be right to ask it.

What do you think your clients experience when you coach them? Complete the exercise in Table 1.1 and then ask clients or fellow coaches to complete the exercise about you too.

Table 1.1 Coach credibility appraisal

	My self-appraisal	Appraisal by others
Body language/posture		
Eye contact		
Voice tone		
Dress/grooming		
Balance of talking vs listening		
Demonstrating interest and asking questions		
Comfort with strong emotions		
Use of stories and anecdotes (overdone/underdone?)		
Energy levels		
Warmth		
Use of humour		
Confidence – personal and professional		
Sharing of personal/professional experiences		
Ability to challenge		
Ability to praise and champion		
Specialist knowledge		
Visibility/profile within coaching industry		
Awards, qualifications, achievements, books, papers		

Comparing all the data, what adjustments could you make to have a more powerful impact and increased credibility? What gaps do you observe? Make a list of actions you might take and work you need to do on the beliefs and assumptions that underpin your current behaviours. Who can support you with this?

My sphere of influence

If you are building a business or even looking to change jobs, research suggests that the best place to start is with your own network of contacts.

Draw a mind map of all the people you know. Start with yourself in the middle and draw lines connecting you to other people in your life. Then draw lines connecting them to people in their lives who could be helpful to you.

Include people who can support you, who are already doing work you would like to do, who inspire you, who have information or knowledge, or who can introduce you to others. Include social media contacts, friends, colleagues, relatives, neighbours and friends from school or university.

Start to notice what a wide sphere of influence you have.

Make a note of the people you could contact and commit to contacting at least one of these people each week to let them know what you are doing or what help and support you are looking for. Ask them what help or support you could offer them in return.

Suggested Further Reading

Coleman, H.J. (1996) *Empowering Yourself: The Organizational Game Revealed.* Dubuque, IA: Kendall/Hunt.

Duckworth, A. (2018) *Grit: The Power of Passion and Perseverance.* New York: Scribner.

Rogers, J. (2017) *Building a Coaching Business: Ten Steps to Success*, 2nd edn. London: Open University Press.

2   Building a Coaching Business

This chapter will encourage you to approach your business like the coach you are and to set yourself clear business objectives. This will involve working 'on' the business and not just 'in' the business. Business planning should be easy for coaches since it entails all the things we do in our coaching role: goal-setting, visioning, designing actions and defining clear outcomes. It will also mean working on your beliefs and your mindset and flexing your behaviour to develop into a business owner, an employer and possibly even a CEO. The great news is that business ownership can be done with a coaching approach, and this chapter will show you how.

If you are reading this book, there is a good chance that you have already set up a coaching business or are getting ready to do so. This chapter is not about the practical details of business start-up, because they are widely available online: from your business banking manager, to the government and organizations like the Federation of Small Businesses or your local Chamber of Commerce. In fact, information and advice about starting a business can be found in abundance and there are also coaches who specialize in how to start a business. There are master's-level courses devoted to running a business and many books aimed specifically at setting up a coaching business (see *Building a Coaching Business: Ten Steps to Success* by Jenny Rogers, 2017). This chapter is not attempting to take the place of in-depth resources about business start-up. Instead it is going to focus on you, your beliefs, your strengths and the things you will need to do that do not involve coaching.

For not only have you had to learn to be a coach, with the myriad of things which that entails, but almost immediately afterwards you also have to learn to be self-employed. It is a lot to ask. As a business owner, you will have many more things to consider besides coaching: finances, marketing, sales, website development, product development, contracts and legal issues, data protection and other compliance requirements, premises, equipment, employment and HR issues. Just as you have to keep reflecting on and developing your coaching skills, so you have to keep reflecting on and developing your business. The start-up phase can be exciting, but your work on the business does not end there.

In the past 20 years, I have seen thousands of coaches graduate from my company's coaching programme and set up their businesses. Some have built highly dynamic and successful companies. Others have struggled in the early stages to make a living but eventually achieved a measure of success. Some coaches tried and failed to establish a coaching business and went back into employment, most of them using coaching as a significant part of their new role. What distinguished the people who made it in self-employment from those who did not? The answer is that it was a variety of factors: how well networked they were, how much of a financial buffer they had, how persistent they were, how 'hungry' they were for business, how well they articulated their services to potential buyers, how much time and energy they put into getting work. It was all those things and more; including some degree of luck, how good they were at coaching was one factor among many, and not necessarily the decisive one.

Being a business owner requires different skills from being a coach. Some might say that some of these skills are diametrically opposed. When you become self-employed, you may have to work hard to develop hitherto underused aspects of yourself and challenge yourself to undertake tasks you thought you were not good at or did not enjoy doing. It can be an exciting new challenge, but it is essential that you go into it with your eyes wide open to the realities of self-employment.

Marketing your Coaching Business

Entrepreneurship is on the increase. Research from StartUp Britain (2016), a government-backed national enterprise campaign, showed 657,796 new businesses were registered in the UK in 2016. This represents a year-on-year growth over the past five years, from 440,600 start-ups in 2011. Coaches are contributing to this increase. In the 2016 ICF Global Coaching Survey (ICF 2016: 68), it was estimated that there are 53,300 freelance coach practitioners worldwide. In the same report, global revenue from coaching was estimated to be US$2.4 billion. The survey also found that self-employed coaches devote on average 17 per cent of their time each week to business development and that the average annual income for a freelance coach is US$51,000. There are conflicting figures about how many start-up businesses fail within the first few years of trading. Some reports suggest as many as 80 per cent but others estimate 40–50 per cent. The sad fact is that a lot of small businesses do not make it. The main reason for failure of the businesses is lack of cash flow, which means quite simply that there is more money going out of the business than there is money coming in.

Setting up a business can be costly and it is tempting to spend not only money, but time, on the visual aspects of your business. I have seen any number of new coaches focus on social media marketing, just like Luke in Case Study 2.1. Having a website and being active on social media give the impression (to you and others) that you have a business. It is a simple fact that you do not have a business if you do not have customers. Social media marketing is a valid and powerful way of raising your profile and attracting clients. However, it needs to be done in conjunction with other kinds of marketing. If you market your business in diverse ways, the chances are that potential customers will start to see your name in several different places, your profile will grow and you will gain credibility.

Rapid fire, scattergun approaches to any kind of marketing are not likely to bring return on investment. There are many companies who use social media successfully as their main source of marketing. They have very clearly identified target markets and a finely tuned social media marketing strategy, which focuses on customer conversion rather than how many shares or likes they get.

Case Study 2.1: Luke

Luke had always dreamed of being self-employed and, after receiving coaching at work, he realized that coaching was what he wanted to do as a career. He completed his training and left his job, full of confidence and anticipation. There had been a lot of coffee-break talk on his coaching course about how much money some coaches earn and Luke was hoping to be one of the successful ones.

He had some savings and spent them on a website and a series of brochures. He loved choosing a name for his business and deciding on images and colours for his branding, and he worked on this for months. Once it was completed, Luke began blogging and spending time on social media and found it fun and a bit addictive to engage with people around the world in this way. He spent a lot of time composing tweets and checking all the social media sites for comments, likes or retweets.

A year after establishing his business, Luke has only had two personal coaching clients, and these did not pay the full rate. He was so keen to secure them as clients that he discounted the prices that he had advertised on his website. Neither of these clients came about from Luke's social media activity and were both personal referrals from his friends. In his first year of trading he has made a significant loss.

Luke feels shocked and disappointed. He realizes that he did not get out and meet any real people but relied entirely on social media to attract clients. He feels as if he has been playing at it. He needs to get some clients and make some money quickly if he is to survive another year, but he does not know how to set about it.

Luke has several options. The good news is that he has a great website and established social media engagement. To get the best from his social media marketing, Luke could access some further training. Additionally, he could develop a list of ideal client personas. This is a fundamental exercise to do when you have a new business. It entails painting a word picture of the different types of clients you are hoping to attract: who they are, where you would find them, how old they are, what they like doing, what problems or issues they have that you could help solve. This enables you to target all your marketing to the people you understand and to whom you can be of service – people who are more likely to be looking for coaching. If Luke continues down the social media marketing route, he needs to become doggedly determined about capturing data and getting newsletter sign-ups. Building a strong database is a vital component of an effective marketing strategy.

Luke also needs to look at his reasons for not getting out and meeting people. Sometimes new business owners do what is safe and comfortable for them and avoid what feels difficult. I have met plenty of new coaches who find it excruciating to do what they see as 'selling themselves'. Even some coaches with a strong sales background can find it a daunting prospect. If you are new to running a business, fear of rejection is something you need to overcome. Along with that comes the need for persistence and resilience. Not everyone will want to become your client, and you have to come to terms with that to be able to carry on selling your services.

There are so many ways to market your business. For a new business owner, it is advisable to find the routes that are most accessible and comfortable for you. You can move into more challenging areas of sales and marketing as you grow in confidence and experience. Aside from social media marketing, other routes include attending networking groups, arranging meetings with prospective clients, writing and giving talks and presentations. What you cannot avoid is actually talking to people about what you do, unless you have a highly sophisticated, targeted online business and social media strategy.

If you have a newly set up coaching business, harness your curiosity and be adventurous in all the ways you engage with prospective clients. This is the engine that will drive your business and you need to attend to it. In other words: 'If you don't drive your business, you will be driven out of business' (Forbes 1915: 230).

Charging for Your Services

Case Study 2.2: Josephine

When she set up her coaching company, Josephine surprised herself and those who knew her by revealing a natural aptitude for selling. She had been a primary school teacher for 25 years and had no experience of business at all, but she joined some business networking groups and developed a great 'elevator pitch' (a persuasive introduction to her company brief enough to be delivered between floors in a lift). As a result, Josephine picked up a lot of one-to-one coaching clients, who were mostly owners of small and medium enterprises (SMEs) from her networking group. Some of them asked Josephine to run some coach training for their teams too. With her teaching background, Josephine was confident about doing this.

Josephine made sure she had meetings with the companies to find out exactly what they wanted, and she tailored each workshop to meet the specific needs of each company. All her clients were happy with the work Josephine did for them. She was working long hours and had little time for the interests she used to have before she started her business, but she was pleased that her clients valued her work. Her clients were referring their friends and colleagues to her and she soon had a waiting list.

When Josephine talked to other coaches about how much they charged, she realized that her fees were comparatively low. When it came to the end of her financial year, she was disappointed to discover that she had only just broken even. She realized that she had spent too much time having meetings with companies and designing and developing workshops. When she divided the fees she received by all the additional hours she had worked on the projects, her hourly rate was pitiful. Josephine was even more crestfallen when one of the companies started to use the workbooks she had developed to train their staff themselves. When Josephine challenged this, the company said that they had understood that the programme had been developed for them and they considered that they had paid for the development and ownership of it too. At this point Josephine realized that she needed to get some information about intellectual property, be clear in her commercial contracts, draw up some terms and conditions and create a realistic pricing structure. She had been naïve about the complexities of charging for her services and developing materials for other people.

One of the golden rules for business owners is to put up your prices when you are in high demand (see Case Study 2.2). If you are turning down opportunities because you are at capacity, it is time to increase your fees. Table 2.1 lists some more indications that it might be time to raise your prices.

The first time someone suggested to me that I raise my prices, I was terrified that I would lose all my clients. I just couldn't bring myself to take the chance, so I decided not to do it. I became busier and more overwhelmed, more resentful and less effective as a coach. I was rushing from place to place and my clients started to seem like revolving doors. My extreme busy-ness was not serving me or my clients. Eventually I nerved myself to put up my prices, held my breath and . . . nothing happened. Everyone accepted the price increase without comment.

If you decide to put up your prices, give your clients as much notice as possible so that they will have time to get used to the change. Let them know the reasons for the price increase too. Be honest about the fact that you are in high demand or that your suppliers have put up their prices and you have had to do the same. If you have won an award, achieved a new qualification or written a book, share the information with your clients in newsletters or social media channels. That way clients will see that you are developing and acquiring new skills, which will reinforce the reason for

Table 2.1 Price rise indicators

Resentment	You are feeling resentful of other coaches who are earning more than you or resentful of the time you spend working. Worse than that, you are starting to feel resentful of your clients.
Timing	You can't remember the last time you increased your fees.
The coaching market	You are currently charging significantly less than your peers in the coaching industry.
Feedback from clients	Your clients are letting you know that they would have paid more for your services.
Overheads	The overheads of running your business have increased. Maybe you have taken on staff or consultants or moved into new premises. Your suppliers have put up their costs. The general cost of living has increased.
Development	You have improved your services, or you have invested in more qualifications for yourself. You know you have more experience and expertise than you did when you started out.
Stagnation	Your working life is like 'Groundhog Day'. It never changes, and you are keen to develop and grow your business. Increased income will give you the opportunity to make improvements.

the price increase. Consumers are used to price increases for all kinds of services and would be surprised to encounter a service for which the price was not raised from time to time.

Many coaches have a rate card for different services and different types of clients. For example, you can have different rates for private, personally funded clients as opposed to corporate sponsored clients. You can have distinct rates for charities, small and medium enterprises (SMEs) and large corporate organizations. You can even include pro bono coaching on your rate card.

If you struggle to charge the appropriate fees, take some time to think about your attitude to money. If you have been a spender, never had any savings and have put a low value on financial security in your personal life, you will probably have the same attitude to your business finances. Similarly, if you have been a worrier about money or a saver in your personal life, you will find the same attitudes showing up in your business. There are specialist financial coaches who can work with you to uncover your beliefs and patterns about finance and to help you approach your business finances with a new attitude. There is also the option of appointing someone to manage the finances of your business if you do not think that you will be able to acquire financial acumen yourself. If you have not considered legal, contractual and compliance issues in setting up your business, ask yourself what stopped you from taking the business of running a business seriously. Commercial contracts are not only a necessary foundation for any business, but they also provide you and others with some clear boundaries about how you will work together. A business owner's focus should include these areas of the business, as well as the more compelling areas, such as coaching itself.

Business Planning

Case Study 2.3: Amanda

Amanda had been self-employed before and therefore business start-up came easily to her. Her previous businesses had been small but successful and Amanda had always been a 'one-woman band'. She had never employed people or had a formal business plan or growth strategy.

Because she was a confident saleswoman, already experienced in business, well-networked and passionate about coaching, her business grew rapidly. After a year Amanda employed a member of staff, and after two years she had three team members. The business was turning over more money than Amanda had ever dreamed of and she was in high demand as a coach and a facilitator.

The business is now five years old and Amanda is not enjoying being a business owner. She is overworked and feels burdened by all the many leadership and administrative tasks she has to deal with. She is still involved in every aspect of the business. She did not begin by writing a business plan or setting clear outcomes, but allowed the business to grow organically, responding to growth without careful thinking.

The staff she appointed a number of years ago were the right fit at the time, but now Amanda needs people with different skills or she needs to find the time to upskill her existing staff. Her current employees have not kept pace with the business growth and members of the team seem to have lost touch with the company's vision. Amanda herself has lost touch with the company's vision as she has been so busy multitasking.

Amanda is confused. The business is booming but she is enjoying it less and less. How can she get herself and her team back on track?

When you are running a business that is growing rapidly, your time is limited and your resources can be stretched to the limit. You are likely to put all your focus into working *in* the business, at the expense of working *on* the business. Without proper planning, you can end up, like Amanda in Case Study 2.3, asking yourself 'How the heck did I end up here, not enjoying myself?'

It is quite common for small business owners to overlook the need for forward planning, and yet planning is essential for your business. In the Department for Business, Innovation and Skills' *Small Business Survey* (2010), obstacles to business success cited by business owners included: the economy, competition, taxation, VAT, PAYE, national insurance, business rates, cash flow, regulations and obtaining finance. Incorporating contingencies in all these areas into a business plan makes sense. A survey by Small Business Trends (2010) showed that having a business plan made you twice as likely to succeed. Lack of planning is regularly cited as a reason for business failure.

The words 'business plan' seem to strike fear into some business owners' hearts. They imagine lengthy, legalistic and wordy documents which are full of complex calculations. This does not have to be the case. Business plans are not intended to be one-off documents, created when you set up and then put away in a file, never to be seen again. They are live, evolving plans, which should be regularly reviewed and revised as your business grows. I review my business plan every year, with the support of a fellow coach. This process involves putting two chairs in front of me. One of them represents my business this time next year, if I have made no changes at all. I sit in the chair and imagine what that will be like, how it will feel and what will be the impact on me, others and the business if things stay the same. Some years I have felt certain that a year without change is exactly what was required to consolidate the business' current position. Other years I have felt disappointed and uncomfortable being in the same place again. Then I move to the other chair which represents the changes I want to have made by this time next year. I sit in it and experience how it will be. From that position, I begin to drill down from the big vision to the key actions I need to take to achieve those changes. At the end of the process I have an action plan, with timescales, specific outcomes and sales targets, which I write down.

I know someone else who draws their business plan and keeps it pinned to their office wall as a visual reminder all year long. Examine your coaching toolkit to see which models or techniques you could use to develop your plan. Choose an approach that will engage you and ignite your desire to plan clearly and imaginatively. Think how often, as coaches, we tell our clients that if they don't know where they are going, they will end up somewhere they may not want to be.

So, follow your coaching principles and, when you set up your business, decide what your end goal is. For example, is your ideal outcome to remain a sole trader with a home-based office, delivering all services yourself, with no employees and no contractors working for you? This option would ensure that you do not have too many responsibilities that could take you away from the core work of coaching. It would also mean that the growth of the business would be limited by the extent of your personal resources. Perhaps your goal is to have premises, staff and associates or consultants. Alternatively, you may be planning to build an online business and create a passive income stream or to build a large consultancy which you want to sell in five or ten years' time. There are many business models. Think about what success would look like for you. Starting with the end in mind will enable you to make the right decisions along the way so that you do not go down other routes that will take you away from your end goal. Be specific in your planning. Do you want to work all over the world or are there limits to how far you will travel? How many hours per day and how many days per week do you want to work? How will you spend your time each week? How much money do you need and want to make from the business each year?

Leadership and growth

Some businesses grow quickly or without planning, like Amanda's in Case Study 2.3. When businesses grow, they can be faced with challenges that cause the business owner stress and leave them feeling unhappy in their work. It can seem as if you are no longer doing what you enjoy or what you are good at. In a fast-growing business, staff can be under pressure to keep up and the owner has to step into a leadership role to support and motivate the team through the transition. Many business owners do not have the leadership skills that this role requires. Many have never led people before and they need to find a way of becoming a leader or appointing someone in the business who can manage the team.

I have spoken to many business owners who started their business with one or two employees with whom they developed close relationships. Sometimes they were more like friends than employees. When the business grows, and decisions need to be made about hiring new staff or letting existing staff go, business owners who have made friends with their staff can struggle to follow through with staff changes. Their blurred boundaries with their employees can sometimes get in the way of what is best for the business.

During times of growth, when more investment is needed, profits can decrease. When services are in high demand and staff are feeling demotivated or uncertain, there is greater chance of errors. Before you can scale up a business, systems need to be in place to support the scaling. In many small businesses, where there are no systems in place to support growth, owners find themselves rushing to set up the necessary infrastructure.

Case Study 2.4: Antonio

Antonio decided to create a detailed five-year step-by-step business plan when he started his coaching business. He had sales targets and key milestones to mark significant achievements in terms of his brand recognition, personal achievements and business growth. He met all his targets and exceeded some. Antonio would often say to others:

'Coaches have the best chance of success in business. They already have all the tools available to them. Starting out with the end in mind and setting goals, with clearly defined action steps, is what coaches do. Why would you not apply all these principles to build your coaching business?'

Antonio in Case Study 2.4 used coaching skills and techniques to build his business. Completing the following exercises will help you to approach your business development from a coaching perspective.

Coaching Exercises for Business Development

Wheel of business focus

In this exercise, each segment of the wheel in Figure 2.1 represents a key area of focus for any business owner. When you are running a business, you have to keep an eye on all these business functions so that you have an understanding of the business as a whole. Use the wheel to identify how much you focus on each area, by giving it a score or marking a line on the segment. Notice where your areas of strength lie and congratulate yourself for your achievements. Turn your attention to those areas which need development. Ask yourself what actions you are prepared to take to improve your focus on those areas. In some cases, you may require additional support or resources.

In this exercise, the wheel in Figure 2.2 is used to explore qualities, traits and behaviours generally found in entrepreneurs. Measure yourself in all the areas on the wheel, and remember to notice how much you are doing, before you focus on areas for development. Work on your own or with a coach to design actions to develop some of the areas that need attention.

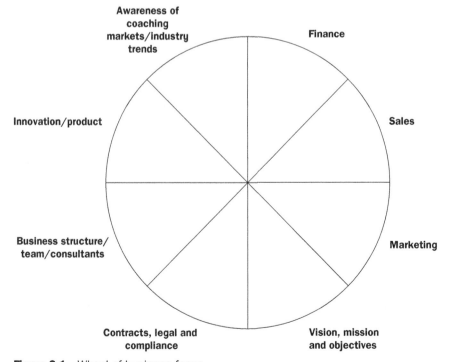

Figure 2.1 Wheel of business focus

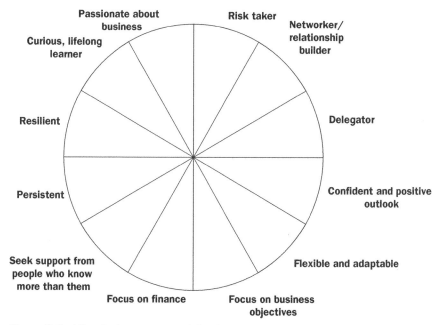

Figure 2.2   Wheel of entrepreneurial traits

Create ideal client avatars

This is a fun exercise for when you are setting up your business. Start by creating a list of your ideal clients. They are likely to be people whose situations you understand, possibly because you have worked with them or even been one of them. Examples of this could be:

- women returning to work after maternity leave
- people who lack assertiveness
- CEOs looking to exit their business
- families who have moved to a new country
- graduates looking for career direction.

Come up with five or six ideal clients. They may be variations on a theme. Now start to bring them to life by filling in the following details about them:

- Who are they?
- What is their age, gender, background, job role, appearance?
- Where would you find them at work?
- Where would you find them in their leisure time?
- What magazines, newspapers or online resources do they read?

- What problems or issues are they facing?
- What do they want?

You can make them even more real by finding photographs from the internet or magazines to represent each of them. You could even draw them if you want.

This exercise will focus your attention on where and to whom you should be marketing your services.

Suggested Further Reading

Brown, C. (2013) *Testing the Water: Helping You Take Your First Steps from Education to Work*. Tollerton, England: Barny Books.

Brown-Volkman, D. (2003) *Four Steps to Building a Profitable Coaching Practice: A Complete Marketing Resource Guide for Coaches*. Lincoln, NE: iUniverse Inc.

Gerber, M.E. (2001) *The E-Myth Revisited: Why Most Small Business Don't Work and What to Do About It*. New York: HarperCollins.

3 Overcoming Impostor Syndrome

The situational impact of starting a new career, often relatively quickly, can also induce something known as Impostor Syndrome in newly qualified coaches who were hitherto confident people. If you are someone who has experienced Impostor Syndrome in other areas of your life, you will not be surprised to learn that the same feelings can transfer to your new role as a coach. This chapter looks at ways to build your confidence and your support network. It will help you to integrate all your previous experiences into your new role as a coach, to assess whether you have done a decent job and to understand that in coaching being a novice can have distinct benefits.

Experiencing Impostor Syndrome

Case Study 3.1: Lauren

Lauren is a great coach – warm, challenging and curious. Since completing her coaching qualification three years ago, Lauren has had only six paying clients. All her other clients have been pro bono. She has had a lot of enquiries for coaching but refers them on to other coaches whom she considers to be more suitable and more experienced than herself. Other delegates from her coaching course and other coaches in her network have benefited from Lauren's referrals. In fact, she has demonstrated an ability to sell anyone other than herself. Lauren has recently engaged a coach to help her address her Impostor Syndrome, which is now affecting her financial situation and her future prospects as a coach. Having made the referrals to other coaches with an apparently good heart, Lauren is now feeling resentful towards these coaches because they have not reciprocated. When she takes an objective assessment of her suitability to coach, she knows that she is as capable as most of the coaches in her network. She knows she has to work on the more deeply held beliefs she has about her own worth.

If you are a newly qualified coach (or even an established coach) and sometimes feel like a fraud, then take comfort from the fact that you are not alone. Many coaches, newly trained or seasoned, can experience Impostor Syndrome (see Case Study 3.1). The term was coined by the clinical psychologists Pauline Clance and Suzanne Imes (1978) to describe the set of feelings and responses they found to be particularly common in successful women. Subsequent studies suggest that up to 70 per cent of people, both men and women, suffer from Impostor Syndrome at some point in their lives. People who experience Impostor Syndrome push themselves hard to compensate for their feelings of inadequacy, often leading to even more success, which in turn results in even greater feelings of being an impostor. They may experience high levels of stress because they are never satisfied with their performance. If you are experiencing Impostor Syndrome as a new coach, you may find yourself fearing that you are going to be 'found out', discounting your successes by putting them down to luck, thinking anyone could do what you do, negating your accomplishments and feeling that you have nothing to offer your clients, comparing yourself unfavourably with other coaches or with your perceptions of other coaches. You may feel like you don't have the right to be doing what you are doing or have a sense that you don't belong where you are. Undervaluing yourself is not a good foundation on which to go out into the world and sell your services.

People who retrain as coaches have typically had careers in other sectors, industries and professions and have built a sense of identity and credibility over a number of years. They have had recognition for what they did both inside and outside of their organization or profession. Quite possibly there had been a progressive route to get there, involving training or academic study, and then a clear career path with defined steps along the way. If you worked hard to achieve a certain status in a previous career, feelings of being a fraud can be triggered by the fact that you got to be a coach relatively quickly and easily in an industry where there is no clear career progression.

Before retraining you may have had an occupation that other people recognized and understood: lawyer, doctor, salesperson, army officer, HR professional or manager. You didn't find yourself being asked, as coaches often are, 'What it is exactly that you do?' Coaching is still a relatively new profession, although it is growing rapidly and much more widely understood than it was in its earlier years. In the 2016 ICF Global Coaching Survey (ICF 2016: 104), participants reported improved general perception of coaching and saw this as an opportunity for coaches. In the *12th Annual Industry Review* by Sherpa Coaching (2017: 29) over 90 per cent of respondents agreed that the credibility of coaching was somewhat or very high. There is no doubt that the coaching industry has matured, but it is not yet universally understood. It can still be challenging to explain it to people who have not experienced coaching, which makes it a harder 'sell' than some more readily understood services or products.

If you used to work in an organization, you will also find yourself without the structure, resources and sense of community that being part of an organization provides. Although you may have longed to see the back of meetings when you left the company, you can feel lonely when they are not happening. In addition, there are no regular appraisals, there is no line manager to support and challenge you and there is no one, other than your clients, to give you feedback. When you start working as a coach it is easy to doubt yourself, wondering if you are doing it well enough or if you are giving your clients what they want when nobody is telling you how good a job you are doing.

Other people train as coaches after having had a career break for some years, usually because they have been working at home, caring for children or family members. Acclimatizing to being back at work after a long break, sometimes with reduced self-confidence, can be a difficult transition, and combining this with starting a business for the first time increases the demands upon you. Taking longer than you expected to establish your business and get paying clients can lead to self-doubt and feelings of being an impostor, particularly if there is additional pressure on you to start earning money quickly.

These are just a few of the factors that make new coaches susceptible to Impostor Syndrome. If you are experiencing Impostor Syndrome as you begin your coaching career, it is worth considering whether this is an unfamiliar feeling brought on by your new role, or a recurrence of something older. Reflect on how many other times in your life you have felt like this. Whether it is new or a repeating pattern, feeling like a fraud is unpleasant and will obstruct you as you work to develop your business.

Real Impostor Syndrome or False Modesty?

If your Impostor Syndrome persists and it is affecting your well-being and your progress, you will need to address it with your coach, therapist or supervisor. Impostor Syndrome may have early childhood origins and is not necessarily a situational response to acquiring a new professional identity in a short space of time. Where you have been a self-professed sufferer of Impostor Syndrome for a long time, it is worth checking with yourself whether your Impostor Syndrome has become a habit behaviour which now serves you in some way. I have encountered coaches who demonstrate false modesty in order to manage the expectations of others and manage their own fear of failure.

Am I Ready to Coach when I Have Just Finished my Training?

Case Study 3.2: Suzy

Suzy qualified as a coach a year ago, having spent the previous 20 years working as a senior HR professional in large corporate organizations. She had taken voluntary redundancy from her last role and decided to invest some of her redundancy money in studying for a recognized coaching qualification. Suzy had always enjoyed the coaching part of

her HR work and had looked forward to leaving behind its less reward-
ing aspects. Although Suzy finished the course on a high, she is now
struggling to believe in herself as a coach and feels like a bit of a fraud.
She had felt confident as an HR professional as she had many years'
experience under her belt but, having completed only a relatively short
course, she cannot believe that anyone would trust her to coach them.
Suzy feels that she needs more experience and knowledge before she
can start coaching paying clients and is wondering whether to do some
further training so that she will feel better equipped to deal with whatever comes up for her clients. 'Why on earth would anyone want me to
coach them when there are so many more experienced and more qualified coaches out there?', she wonders.

If, like Suzy in Case Study 3.2, you find it hard to trust that you have sufficient experience or training to start coaching and charging for it, you might take time to
consider all your previous professional and life experiences and work on appreciat-
ing what they have contributed to you becoming a coach. When you find yourself in
a classroom after many years, it is easy to feel deskilled and incompetent. You may
be inclined to discount all you have done before as inconsequential or irrelevant to
the new skill you are learning. But it is important to remember that coaching is an
adult learning experience and adult learning relies on learners bringing their own
experiences and opinions to the training. One of the underpinning principles of
adult learning is that, as we mature, we accumulate a growing reservoir of experience which becomes a resource for future learning. Indeed, coaching is one of the
few professions in which life experience – and even a few grey hairs – are considered to be an advantage, if not a necessity.

Coaching is not like other, more established, professions – it is still emerging
and developing, and in some senses it continues to be uncharted territory. As coaching has evolved, it has drawn on knowledge and theories from a wide range of dis-
parate disciplines to inform the practice – from psychology through to business,
organizational and leadership models, therapy and the self-help movement. Coaching builds on your existing skillsets and your previous work and life experiences.

We develop our knowledge of coaching as evidence-based practitioners. That
means that our work consists of bringing together the skills and theory we have
acquired when we encounter a client. It may be a different cocktail of theory, practice and skills with each client. In my work with a university, teaching a work-based
learning approach to coaching, we consider that coaches are informing the wider
practice of the industry as they develop their own approaches, theories and skills.
I think that is an exciting place to be.

It is likely that you will have chosen to train as a coach because you enjoy supporting and developing others, have good people skills, demonstrate empathy and
are not judgemental. You almost certainly made the choice to be a coach because
you felt you were playing to your existing strengths and to your interests. You may

have even found that before training as a coach you were instinctively using certain approaches in your coaching, and that the training programme affirmed what you had been doing before and gave your intuitive methodology a structure and some underpinning theory. Any professional and accredited coach training organization will also have assessed your suitability to undertake the programme, based on your experience, attitude and aptitude.

Value what you are bringing to the profession from your previous experiences. Enjoy your curiosity and remember that a state of not-knowing is a prerequisite to coaching. A coach does not need to know the answers. Your role is to provide the conditions, whatever they are for the individual client in front of you, that will enable them to think about their lives in a meaningful way. Becoming a coach is probably the culmination of years of experience of life and work and did not just happen on your coach training programme.

How do I Know if I am Doing a Decent Job?

Case Study 3.3: Alison

Alison has been coaching for nine months but has a constant feeling that she is not doing enough for her clients. She does not think that she is delivering anything of real value, as she expected her clients to have more 'light bulb' moments during coaching. Often her sessions feel to Alison like a nice chat and no more than that. In her worst moments she suspects that her clients keep coming to see her only because they are not assertive enough to tell her that the coaching sessions are not meeting their expectations. For this reason, Alison avoids asking her clients for feedback and has started to offer them additional sessions free of charge. She often leaves a coaching session berating herself for not having thought of the 'right' questions or used the appropriate tools or techniques. She describes herself as a 'rabbit in the headlights' when she is coaching and often sends her clients homework and reading between sessions to add extra value when she has had time to reflect. She is worried about being 'found out', and imagines that other coaches have a powerful impact on their clients, enabling them to undergo significant transformations.

Like Alison in Case Study 3.3, many new coaches worry whether they have done enough for their clients. I have even heard some coaches wonder whether they are doing anything useful at all. This raises several questions:

- Have they contracted effectively with their clients so that outcomes have been identified for the coaching sessions?

- Are they asking their clients for feedback?
- How much do they understand the change process?
- Whose agenda are they working towards?
- How much value are they giving to the fact that the coaching session is a time and space for the client to think in a safe and confidential environment?
- What expectations do they have about coaching sessions and where did these expectations come from?

Let us look at some simple steps for determining whether you have done a good job as a coach. These are:

- Contract, contract, contract
- Learn to read your client
- Testimonials and referrals
- Manage your own expectations about change

Contract, contract, contract

Contract and re-contract throughout the coaching sessions. That means determining at the start what your client wants to achieve from the coaching overall and, as the coaching progresses, from each session. Remember that coaching outcomes don't have to be actions. Outcomes can be changes in attitude, feelings or beliefs. They can even be aspirations or resolutions, such as a promise to oneself to make time to think and take stock. Check in with your client midway through each session to make sure you are on track with what the client wants, and allow time to review how far your client achieved their objective for the session. Accept that sometimes your client's goals or objectives will change, so check with them at the start of every session and be ready to contract about some different outcomes as the coaching sessions take new twists and turns.

If you are coaching in an organization, the same contracting process will apply but you are likely to be contracting with the organization as well as the individual coachee. If this is the case, you will begin the coaching assignment with a three-way meeting between the coachee and their line manager or coaching sponsor. The purpose of the three-way meeting is to agree outcomes from an organizational and individual perspective for the coachee. You may have a review midway through the coaching assignment and will finish with a final three-way meeting to reflect on how far the objectives have been achieved. You can read more about conducting a three-way meeting in Chapter 4.

Learn to read your client

The easiest way to know if the coaching sessions are working for your client is to notice what is happening for them within the session and more generally. Do you see evidence of change or progress? How engaged is your client in the coaching process and in completing any additional work in their own time? Watch and listen for feedback that may not be explicitly expressed. If you are a coach, you will have been trained to observe non-verbal signals and to notice the subtleties of your client's language. Notice inconsistencies between spoken words and body language or behaviours. Hear what is said and what is not said. Follow your hunches and check with your client if you feel that a tool or technique or an aspect of the coaching session is not working for them.

Experience each client as a wonderful and unique human being and learn to understand how they exhibit different emotional states. For example, some people are visibly excited and vociferous if they have a new insight, while others sit still and give little away. For some, moments of profound transformational learning can occur very quietly. Do not make the mistake of interpreting your client's response by some universal measure of behaviour. The way your client shows their appreciation of the coaching you provide will differ enormously from one person to the next. If your Impostor Syndrome starts to run rife, you may misread your client's signals and you will make everything you see and hear fit your belief that you are not good enough. If you can't bring your Impostor Syndrome under control, you will need to seek supervision or coaching to deal with it. If you don't, it will seriously undermine your efficacy as a coach, your own well-being and your business. I know some coaches who wear their Impostor Syndrome as a 'badge of honour' and I feel uncomfortable about this. As coaches, we have a duty to our clients to show that we are self-aware enough to acknowledge our vulnerabilities but self-motivated enough to work on addressing them.

Testimonials and referrals

Ask for testimonials and referrals from clients and organizations at the end of coaching assignments. If they are forthcoming and positive, then believe them. Keep all feedback and testimonials somewhere easily accessible so that you can reread them whenever you need a confidence boost. Don't just think about doing this, either. As a coach, you know that developing confidence and overcoming Impostor Syndrome require work. Notice any themes emerging in feedback or testimonials you have received and acknowledge that if several of your coachees have noticed the same qualities in you, then it is likely that those qualities are there for all to see. Keep a log of all your coaching sessions too. This is often required by your accrediting body anyway, but it will also be a visual reminder for you of all the coaching you have done, the successes you have had and how many of your coachees have returned for more.

Manage your own expectations about change

Manage your expectations about changes you will see and accept that few coaching sessions contain transformational moments. Remind yourself how change happens and how many hidden competing commitments keep clients tethered to their familiar beliefs and behaviours. Bringing about change through coaching is a long and complex game, at the root of which is a relationship of trust and respect between coach and client.

If you are in a hurry to see transformation in your clients, you will unconsciously, or perhaps even consciously, communicate this to them. This will put pressure on them and may make them feel that they are letting you down by not changing quickly enough. Alternatively, it may cause them to become resistant to you and, therefore, to changing. Working with ease, not urgency, is essential in building the coaching relationship and creating the right conditions for your client to feel safe enough to explore new thoughts and behaviours.

Timothy Gallwey (1974) suggests that: 'Ideally, the end of every coaching session is that the client leaves feeling more capable of mobility.' If you have achieved some shift, however small, in your client's thinking or awareness at the end of a coaching session, you have made significant progress.

How to Build Confidence, Support and Experience as a Coach

If you have a pinch of Impostor Syndrome, remember that it is useful to accept that you are a novice coach and that you still have more to learn and more experience to gain. It is probably, on balance, better to question your competence as a coach than to overestimate it. The opposite of Impostor Syndrome is the belief that you are much more competent than you are, leading to a refusal to acknowledge your limitations. This cognitive bias was identified by the Cornell University psychologist David Dunning and his student, Justin Kruger. In 'Unskilled and Unaware of It: How Difficulties in Recognizing One's Own Incompetence Lead to Inflated Self-Assessments', the authors suggest that you need skill and knowledge to be able to determine how skilled and knowledgeable you are (Kruger and Dunning 1999). The less competence a person has, the more likely they are to overestimate their abilities (see Case Study 3.4). This is known as the Dunning–Kruger effect. People with high levels of ability, in contrast, tend to assume that what comes easily to them must also be easy for others, so they are more likely to undervalue their own talents.

Case Study 3.4: Dave

Dave experienced no Impostor Syndrome whatsoever. He completed a short coach training course and didn't bother to get any professional accreditation. He wanted to be the next big 'name' in coaching and he wanted it quickly. He had spent time with coaches who claimed that they charged big money for their coaching sessions and Dave expected to do the same, and immediately. He made grand claims on his website about how he could change lives quickly. Deep down, Dave had good intentions. He had turned around his own life and wanted to share his story with others. He set out to be an internationally renowned motivational speaker. Dave invested huge sums of money in promoting himself, but he didn't ever achieve the success he craved. He showed no humility or vulnerability and didn't demonstrate a coaching approach to people. He didn't continue to learn about himself or about coaching. He talked at people, rather than listened to them. He overestimated himself and underestimated others, and people saw in him what was maybe a bit of the Dunning–Kruger effect. Dave eventually gave up on his dream, blaming the world for 'not being ready for him'.

As a newly trained coach you are much more likely to experience Impostor Syndrome than to exhibit the Dunning–Kruger effect. You may find it useful to appraise your level of confidence (from low to high) and your degree of competence (from none to expert) and then determine how you can increase both competence and confidence in equal measure.

It will help to attend regular training days, CPD sessions or webinars on coaching or coaching-related topics. If you are a member of a professional coaching body, CPD attendance will be a requirement for you to maintain your accreditation or credentials. Now you have entered the coaching profession, you will need to keep pace with its rapid development and continue your reading about coaching by subscribing to coaching and coaching-related magazines, journals and online publications. The commitment to ongoing learning can be a surprise to some newly trained coaches. Coach training programmes often require a considerable financial investment and some coaches are unwilling or unable to commit to further ongoing training until they have generated regular income from their coaching work. Some coach training companies offer ex-students the opportunity to assist on future coach training programmes. Going through aspects of your training again from the perspective of helper on the programme can build your confidence and embed your learning.

Supervision

Some newly qualified coaches think there is no point accessing coaching supervision until they have some clients to discuss with a supervisor. Actually, supervision and CPD are essential if you are to feel competent and confident as a coach, and you don't need to have clients to have supervision. If your finances are stretched, look for low-cost ways of accessing support, practice and further learning. For instance, many coaches find co-coaching or peer coaching sessions helpful in developing their practice – and these are usually either free of charge or cost very little. Seeing how other people coach, being on the receiving end of coaching and getting honest feedback from other coaches support your development and build your confidence and competence. It is a good idea to join a coaching network so that you can mix with both new and experienced coaches and meet coaches who have been trained by a different coaching provider or with a different approach to coaching.

Whether you call it coaching supervision, mentor coaching or meta-coaching, spending time reflecting on your coaching practice with a skilled, professional thinking partner is an essential element of the development of your confidence and competence as a coach. All of us, whatever our occupation, think and function better with a skilled, professional thinking partner dedicating their time and expertise to our development and well-being. In this respect coaches are no different from other professionals. Whatever type of coach you are – a team leader who coaches, an internal coach or a freelance coach – regular access to a trained supervisor or mentor coach is indispensable to your development. A supervisor/mentor coach is someone who can help you work through your thought processes, develop your coaching capability, challenge any limiting beliefs and assumptions, and champion you when you need it.

Supervision or mentor coaching offers a disproportionately positive return on investment and helps you maintain continuous and rigorous self-reflection. It provides a framework and space that enable you to gain necessary perspective on your work and to talk through more complex issues arising for you with your clients. You can work through ethical issues in confidence and consider the wider implications of the coaching work, including the organizational perspective, with the support of a more experienced practitioner. A skilled supervisor will also help you to identify and address the aspects of your own behaviours that might get in the way of your effectiveness as a coach.

I can usually recognize coaches who have not extended their development beyond their initial coach training experience. Coaching can become formulaic, and self-awareness limited, if coaches do not commit to ongoing personal and professional development. It is through supervision, CPD and peer coaching that much of a coach's development takes place, and therefore supervision is integral to the effectiveness of the work done during coaching.

Our role as coaches is to encourage self-reflection in our clients, to create awareness and ignite our clients' thinking in order to help greater understanding emerge:

> Awareness is like the glow of a coal, which comes from its own combustion: what is given by introspection is like the light reflected from an object when a flashlight is turned on it.
>
> (Perls, Hefferline and Goodman 1951: 75)

Developing and growing as a coach also mean becoming a reflective practitioner about your own work. Reflection requires an open mind, asking 'What if', viewing things from an unfamiliar perspective and thinking about the consequences of your choices in a process of continuous learning.

The Benefits of Being a Novice

Remember that there are also benefits to being a novice. You are likely to be full of enthusiasm and curiosity, and because of your limited experience of coaching people, you are necessarily in the 'state of not-knowing' about your clients, which – as mentioned previously – is a prerequisite to good coaching. A perpetual challenge for coaches is to remain in a state of not-knowing, as being in the role of 'expert' can lead coaches to diagnose and find solutions, which may not be what the client needs. After 25 years as a coach, I am ashamed to confess that I sometimes find myself thinking 'I've seen this before and I know just what is going on', which could lead to missing crucial observations. Patrick Casement (1985: 4) sums this up in his book about the therapeutic relationship, *On Learning from the Patient*:

> It is all too easy to equate not knowing with ignorance. This can lead thera-
> pists to take refuge in an illusion that they understand. But if they can bear
> the strain of not-knowing, they can learn that their competence as therapists
> includes a capacity to tolerate feeling ignorant or incompetent and a willing-
> ness to wait (and to carry on waiting) until something genuinely relevant and
> meaningful begins to emerge ... By listening too readily to accepted theo-
> ries, and to what they lead the practitioner to expect, it is easy to become
> deaf to the unexpected. When a therapist thinks that he can see signs of what
> is familiar to him, he can become blind to what is different and strange.

In the 1970s, Noel Burch, of the US organization Gordon Training International, developed a model known as the Conscious Competence Framework based on four stages of learning (Burch 1970s). The framework illustrates how we move through increasing levels of awareness and capability as we acquire a new skill.

The first stage is Unconscious Incompetence: We don't know what we don't know, and
    we don't even know that we need to know it.
The second stage is Conscious Incompetence: This stage is reached when we start
    learning something for the first time and we become acutely aware of our own
    lack of skill.
The third stage is Conscious Competence: We have been learning to do something and
    we now know that we have the skills to do it, but we still have to think about what
    we are doing and how we are doing it. It doesn't quite come naturally but we are
    consciously aware of what we need to do.
The final stage is Unconscious Competence: We take it for granted that we can do it,
    almost without thinking about it.

The analogy often used to illustrate these four stages is one of learning to drive, but I also think a powerful analogy is training to be a coach. Each of the stages has its benefits and its downsides.

When you are a newly trained coach you are probably at the stage of conscious competence, and the benefits to this are that you are unlikely to slip into complacency or to think that you 'know'. You will apply yourself with care and tenacity to your work.

Using Impostor Syndrome as a Coaching Niche?

If you are a coach who has experienced Impostor Syndrome and you have found a way of managing it, why not turn it to your advantage and make it one of your areas of expertise? It's always easier to write blogs and articles or deliver presentations with conviction and authenticity about something you have experienced yourself. Clients will feel that you understand them if you have experienced what they are going through. This will tend to normalize their experience, which will make change more likely for them. Jack Mezirow (1991) identified a number of factors or situations which give rise to transformational learning and change. One of the factors was 'recognizing that others share our feelings'. Knowing that you have found strategies for dealing with your own feelings of inadequacy will give your clients evidence that change is possible. With an estimated 70 per cent of people experiencing Impostor Syndrome, you should not be short of clients.

Coaching Exercises for Dealing with Impostor Syndrome

Build an evidence wall

Picture your favourite police/crime drama on television. There is always a wall in the police station covered with photographs, dates, names and evidence to help the detectives solve the crime. You can tackle your Impostor Syndrome in exactly the same way – by building an evidence wall to dispute your internal claim that you are a fraud, have only got where you are because of luck and that none of your achievements have much meaning. Pauline Clance (1985) used three measures to test the extent of Impostor Syndrome in her research subjects:

- Fake (to what extent they felt others would find them out as a fake)
- Discount (to what extent they discounted praise from others)
- Luck (to what extent they externalized their successes)

On a wall in your office or on a large pinboard, start to create your own evidence wall to refute your Impostor Syndrome. Include testimonials, work you have completed, jobs you have held down, offers of work you have had. Also include personal qualities, strengths and skills you have, as well as training and education you have undertaken and your family, social and household responsibilities.

When you have completed it, step back and look with fresh eyes at all that you are and all that you have achieved for yourself and others. Notice what you are doing today that you couldn't have done five or ten years ago. Acknowledge your progress and, looking at your evidence wall, consider whether you are capable and worthy of coaching others.

Write your own reference

Complete the following reference for yourself for a coaching assignment (without false modesty and with as much enthusiasm, generosity and kindness as you would use if writing a reference for a fellow coach in whom you believe). You can refer to professional and personal experiences or qualities in the reference in Table 3.1.

Table 3.1   Write your own reference

Name
Greatest personal qualities and strengths
Greatest professional qualities and strengths
Words others use to describe them
I have total confidence in recommending them because
Their top five successes and achievements are

Suggested Further Reading

Cuddy, A. (2016) *Presence: Bringing Your Boldest Self to Your Biggest Challenges.* London: Orion Publishing.

Goyder, C. (2014) *Gravitas: Communicate with Confidence, Influence and Authority.* London: Vermillion.

Watts, G. and Morgan, K. (2015) *The Coach's Casebook: Mastering the Twelve Traits That Trap Us.* Cheltenham: Inspect & Adapt Ltd.

4 Contracting, Pitching and Client Meetings

When you were training to be a coach, you probably learned about 'chemistry' sessions, three-way meetings with corporate client organizations, contracting sessions and how to pitch your services to clients. It is possible that you paid less attention to this part of your training than to the theory and practice of coaching and the practice sessions you did with your fellow students. I have noticed this to be true of some of my own students. This chapter is intended to help you prepare for the various meetings you will need to attend as a self-employed coach and to encourage you to think about your strategies for making the most of these opportunities.

The Business of Coaching

Sometimes it can be a surprise to new self-employed coaches to discover that they are not spending most of their time coaching. Coaches need to invest a lot of time and energy in their business development: marketing, social media, writing, developing programmes or workshops, giving talks, networking, meeting potential clients and bidding for work. Even when a business opportunity starts to materialize, you will probably have several more hoops to jump through before you can start doing what you signed up for: coaching. The lead-in time for a piece of work to materialize is probably longer when you are working with corporate clients than when you are working with individuals. The administrative wheels of organizations tend to move slowly, and I have heard many new coaches announce to me excitedly that they have secured some organizational coaching work, only to hear from them again several months later that it has not yet been officially approved. In my organization, we have sometimes waited for as long as two years to start a piece of work with a company. Lots of factors can contribute to the time lapse: budgetary constraints, changes in organizational strategy, your contact in the organization moving to another role or company, other business activities taking priority. When you have first set up your business, the time lapse between winning the work and the work starting can make you disheartened and frustrated – particularly if you are financially dependent on this piece of work.

If you were a self-employed consultant before you added coaching to your offering, you will be more familiar with the length of the sales cycle and the need to have client meetings before work can begin. As a newly self-employed person you will quickly gain experience, but it can be challenging to have these meetings without having had a practice run first.

Three-Way Meetings

If you are coaching in organizations, you may be involved in three-way or triad meetings with both the person who is going to be coached by you and the corporate sponsor of the coaching. Ideally, there should be a session or part of a session dedicated to contracting with all your clients and there may be additional contracting with corporate sponsors too. If you are bidding for work, you may have to submit written proposals or tenders and, if you get through to the second stage, you will probably be invited to a panel interview or to give a presentation about your company and your proposal.

The three-way meeting is an important part of the coaching assignment in that it brings together the key people who are going to be involved in the coachee's personal and professional development. These are: the coachee, the coach and the coachee's line manager or other sponsor of coaching, who may be someone with an HR role in the organization. You will already have a commercial contract in place with the organization, which covers practicalities such as payment terms and cancellation charges, but the three-way meeting provides an opportunity to have a different type of contracting conversation with the organization. The meeting should cover:

- The purpose of the coaching
- The process and objectives of the coaching
- How progress and success will be measured and recognized
- Lines of reporting, feedback mechanisms, boundaries and confidentiality
- Roles and responsibilities
- What support will be given and by whom

It is your role as coach to lead and facilitate the meeting and to explain clearly the purpose and the benefits of the three-way meeting and contracting process. You will need to set the scene and position this meeting as a positive and valuable experience (see Case Studies 4.1 and 4.2).

Case Study 4.1: Alice

Alice worked as an HR Business Partner for seven years in a large organization. Part of her role included being an internal coach. She completed an accredited in-house coach training programme and attended in-house supervision and coaching development workshops. The internal coaching was limited to specific coaching programmes: *Transition*

Coaching from Manager to Leader and *Career Coaching* for delegates on the graduate programme. Anyone having coaching in the organization was assigned a coach. There was no selection process and no chemistry meeting. There was also no three-way meeting with the person being coached and their line manager or other organizational sponsor.

Alice always planned to leave the company and set up as a freelance coach, as this was the aspect of her work that she enjoyed most. She managed her exit carefully, saving money so that she had a financial buffer which would give her two years' grace to establish her business. She also let all her corporate contacts know that she would be setting up her own business and that she would be interested in providing coaching for them. This proved to be a successful strategy and Alice has been offered numerous opportunities for one-to-one leadership and executive coaching.

Most of the organizations who offered Alice coaching work expected her to attend a three-way meeting at the start of each coaching assignment to establish goals and outcomes for the sessions, and then to attend a three-way review meeting at the end of the coaching assignment to reflect on how far the objectives had been met. Having now completed a few three-way meetings, Alice does not feel that they went well or that they were useful to any of the three parties. The line managers of the people being coached were not able to spend much time discussing the coaching programme and most of the meetings have been brief conversations that merely identified some organizational goals for the coaching sessions. Alice feels sure that these meetings could be more productive and is keen to know how they should be conducted, as she has no previous experience to draw on and has so far launched herself into them without much planning.

One of the findings of the *6th Ridler Report* (Mann 2016: 61) was that 75 per cent of the 105 participating organizations encourage line managers to review coaching objectives in three-way meetings. However, in practice I have seen the three-way meeting treated in a cursory way by all three parties, as if it is merely a formal requirement rather than an intrinsic part of the process. Conducting a three-way meeting with the same level of care, attention and preparation that you give your coaching sessions will give a message that the investment the organization is making in providing coaching for their employee is something to be honoured and valued. You will also be presenting yourself to the organization and the individual being coached as a credible coach who has clear boundaries and professional values. You will need to model coaching skills in the meeting: listening, clarifying and summarizing, demonstrating understanding and asking powerful questions. The conversation should be facilitated using adult-to-adult communication and lack of bias in your communications with both parties. It is an opportunity for you to make a favourable impression on the coaching sponsor and to give sponsor and coachee a positive and powerful experience of coaching.

Ideally, the three-way meeting will take place after the chemistry session and after your initial one-to-one contracting discussion with the client, in which you will have been able to explain the purpose and process of the three-way meeting. Coachees often have goals for the coaching that they are happy to share and agree with their line manager, but they also have private goals that they will share with the coach but not with their manager or the organization. Private goals may be about personal aspects of the coachee's life, such as their health and fitness, finances, family issues or relationships. They may also be about wanting to improve relationships with individuals at work. Sometimes coachees want to work on improving their relationship with their line manager, but do not want this goal to be shared.

It is useful to have an agenda for the three-way meeting, which can be printed or simply discussed with the attendees. Here is a suggested outline for a three-way meeting, with suggested topics and questions. This is not a list of questions to be worked through systematically, but intended to give you an idea of the sorts of questions you could ask under each topic:

- Introduction
- The background to the coaching assignment
- Coaching objectives
- Feedback and confidentiality
- Discussion of measurement
- Conclusion

Introduction

The coach explains the purpose of the meeting and gives a brief reminder of the role of the coach and what coaching is and is not.

The background to the coaching assignment

What has given rise to the request for coaching? How committed is the client to having coaching and making it work? How committed is the line manager to supporting the coachee? What form of support would the client like to have from the manager?

Coaching objectives

What are the coachee's public goals for the coaching? What are the goals of the line manager and the organization's goals? What is already working? What change are they looking for? What would it look like, sound like and feel like if the coaching was really successful? What outcomes would they like to see? What could get in the way of achieving these outcomes? What will happen if the outcomes are not met or if the goals need to be reviewed?

Feedback and confidentiality

How will feedback on the coaching sessions be managed? Who will update the line manager on progress? What will be the limits of the updates in terms of content (with reference to public goals)? Where are the limits of confidentiality in the coaching relationship?

Discussion of measurement

How will success be measured, and by whom?

Conclusion

The coach restates the key points that have been agreed on and brings the meeting to a close.

Later, you may want to write up these key points and distribute them to the participants. After the line manager has left the three-way meeting, there will be an opportunity for you and the coachee to discuss private goals, which will not be shared with the organization. It is worth mentioning that in the last five to seven years, organizations have become more informed about managing the three-way process. I remember occasions in the past when line managers phoned me, without the coachee's knowledge, with the intention of finding out how the coaching was going or of giving me information about the coachee. Today the evidence suggests that only 10 per cent of organizations encourage line managers to speak to the coach without the coachee present (*Ridler Report,* Mann 2016: 61).

Even if you do not have a three-way meeting, it is still important for you to discuss organizational goals with your client organization and to maintain an explicit awareness of the organizational context in which the coaching is being delivered.

Case Study 4.2: Hope

Hope uses three-way meetings to understand more about the wider system surrounding the coachee. She asks the coachee and their line manager or sponsor to describe their current relationship in metaphorical terms. For example, if their relationship were a book or a film, which one would it be? She encourages the line manager to make some appreciative statements about the coachee and then invites the coachee to do the same about their manager.

Hope often takes a bag of pebbles with her and asks manager and coachee to use the stones to represent their wider team. She invites them to position the pebbles according to the relationships and dynamics within the team. Hopes asks coachee and manager to identify what or who in the wider system could either support or hinder the coaching process. She ends the three-way session with some agreed outcomes for the coaching. These have been informed by the coaching session which she has facilitated with both parties.

The impact of Hope's three-way meetings is always positive. Both parties feel engaged and connected to each other and to the coaching process. The meetings are memorable, meaningful and give both people an experience of what it is like to be coached by Hope. Line managers who have been involved in three-way meetings with Hope often contact her at a later date to ask her to be their coach.

Contracting with One-to-One Clients

Contracting does matter: many of the practical or ethical dilemmas which coaches bring to my supervision sessions come down to a lack of clear contracting. I have met many coaches who sheepishly admit that they gloss over the contracting conversation. The contracting discussion in a coaching relationship is arguably the most important one that you will have with your client. It sets the scene for what is to come in the relationship and ensures that you lay a firm foundation, clarifying mutual expectations and enabling you and your client to discuss how you are going to work together.

Remember that new clients probably don't know how the process of coaching works – and even if they have some awareness, they will not know as much as you do about how you work as a coach. Clients come to coaching ready to learn from you about how you will work together. They may be feeling vulnerable, worried or unsure, and letting them know at the beginning what they can expect from the process provides them with certainty and security.

A clear contracting process allows you to sort out all the necessary procedural details so that the client's concerns can become the main focus of attention. It provides a safe container, a firm foundation for the professional relationship, and clarifies mutual expectations (see Case Study 4.3). Clients who have experienced little or no formal contracting from their coach will feel unsafe and unclear throughout the process. Along with the three-way meeting, this is one of the few times that you will need to take control of the process, albeit with a coaching approach.

Case Study 4.3: Hayley

Hayley would be the first person to admit that she was not interested in learning about contracting when she completed her training as a coach. She is a spontaneous and trusting person herself and did not feel comfortable being overly formal with her clients before she had even started to coach them. She was worried that it would break the trust and rapport which she had created with them when they first met. Hayley's contracting consisted of less than five minutes at the start of the first coaching session, in which she talked about confidentiality and the duration and frequency of the sessions. Then she got going with the coaching.

Now that Hayley has been coaching for a couple of years, she has learned the importance of formal contracting. She had several tricky situations with her clients because they had not fully understood the rules of engagement from the start. One client began phoning Hayley for ad hoc coaching every couple of days, and was eventually disappointed when Hayley explained that this was not acceptable and was not any part of the coaching agreement. But what agreement? They did not have one. Hayley thought it was implicitly understood that her support was confined to the coaching sessions. However, she remembered that she had said in conversation that she was available by phone or email if the client needed her between sessions. She realized that this was open to different interpretations and that she needed to set clearer boundaries and establish less ambiguous expectations. Hayley also had difficulties with clients not turning up for sessions and not knowing that they had to pay for missed sessions as this had not been explicitly discussed either.

Hayley is now looking to build contracting sessions into her coaching practice and to provide a written contract too.

How to contract

The contracting can take place immediately before the first coaching session or it can be a separate session a week or so before. Some coaches build in an additional 30 minutes at the start of the first coaching session and others have a distinctly separate intake session that includes contracting. Professional coaching bodies such as the ICF list contracting as one of their core competencies and they expect their members to have clear contracting conversations and provide written contracts. If you are a member of a professional coaching body, you will be familiar with requirements about contracting. Sample coaching contracts are provided by many coach training providers and coaching bodies.

The contract covers several aspects:

Logistics: duration of sessions, timing and frequency; fees and cancellations; contact between sessions; venue.

Boundaries: confidentiality; roles, responsibilities and expectations; conflicts of interest.

Ways of working: face to face, phone or Skype; coaching methodologies; outcomes; measurements of success; preparation or work between sessions.

Your professional practice: membership of coaching bodies, code of practice, code of ethics, insurances, supervision.

Coaching is a complex and dynamic process and is more than the sum of its parts. The elements of a coaching contract can be adapted, revisited or expanded throughout a coaching relationship as the relationship and its complexities reveal themselves. But if you started the relationship with a clear contract, it will be much easier for either you or the client to revisit the contract if any potential areas of misunderstanding or conflict arise.

By formally contracting with individual clients, you will be establishing yourself as a credible professional who holds the client's safety and well-being as paramount.

Pitches, Proposals and Presentations

Case Study 4.4: Christine

Christine is an experienced coach who has developed two clear coaching offerings: one-to-one leadership/executive coaching and workshops on coaching skills for managers. Most of Christine's work comes from word-of-mouth recommendation so she has never had to pitch her services to an organization. She appreciates how fortunate she is that work has come to her so easily. Recently Christine was contacted by an organization and asked to submit a proposal for a series of Manager as Coach training programmes. The organization has now invited Christine to a panel interview where she has been asked to deliver a presentation about her proposal. Christine feels nervous. It is a big piece of work and could make a difference to her income for the next two years if she wins the business. Christine does not consider herself much of a saleswoman and has developed her business by building personal relationships. She knows she struggles to promote herself and she always panics when people ask her 'Why should I choose you over other coaches?' She is looking for guidance on how to approach this sort of meeting.

When you become a coach, you can find yourself undertaking all kinds of new and unanticipated tasks. Pitching your services to organizations might be one of them. It takes practice, time and energy to do it well. New coaches who have a background in sales seem to win a lot of high-value business in organizations, because they know how to do it, and are therefore confident. New coaches with no sales background tend to concentrate on winning personal clients first until they build the confidence and skills needed to pitch on a larger scale to an organization. If, like Christine in Case Study 4.4, you lack experience in giving presentations or in selling, you could consider doing some additional training in these areas as you will need these skills in your coaching career.

There is no one right way to approach making a pitch or a presentation to sell your services because every situation is unique, and every coach will have a different approach, but there are some guidelines which can help you plan your own approach.

Preparation

> By failing to prepare, you are preparing to fail.
>
> (sometimes attributed to Benjamin Franklin).

In the context of making a pitch, preparation means several things. It means practising what you are going to say on your own and maybe in front of a group of trusted advisors – people who you know will give you honest feedback. It also means doing some research. Find out as much as you can about the organization, right down to what the dress code is and what the company values are. Plan to wear something that fits with the company culture.

Learn the terms the organization uses for training interventions, which may be different from the words you use. For example, you may call the people on the programme 'delegates' but the organization refers to them as 'participants'. Get to know what they call their existing programmes too. I once referred to an organization's 'Parents' Network' and was quickly informed that it is called a 'Family Network'. As soon as this happened, I felt a subtle cooling in the rapport I had built with the panel. Another time I referred to a local police force as 'the force'. Luckily, they found it highly amusing and told me that they preferred to say 'the organization'. Using an organization's own language builds rapport and shows them that you understand them. This makes it more likely that they will trust you to deliver a programme or workshop that has the right style, tone and content to fit with their own culture.

Find out as much as you can about the meeting, interview or pitch that you have been invited to attend. For example, if you have responded to a tender for work, the process is likely to be more formal. There is also likely to be a difference in the level of formality of the process depending on whether you are meeting a small company, a large multinational, a not-for-profit organization or a public-sector body. Contact the organization in advance to find out how much they are able to tell you about the interview. Put yourself in the shoes of the buyers of coaching before you go to the meeting. What would you be looking for? What would you be worried about? It is likely that the buyers of coaching services will have negotiated hard for a budget for coaching interventions and they will want to find the right supplier who will deliver excellent value. The people you are meeting may even have put their own reputations on the line within the organization to secure a coaching budget, so the personal stakes may be high for them. If you have been a buyer of training or coaching services in the past, remind yourself what you wanted to see, hear and experience when someone was pitching to you. If you have never been in this position, talk to someone you know who is, and ask them for advice.

Tell stories

Use anecdotes and real-life examples to illustrate what you are saying and to offer evidence of the way you work. Talk about other clients you have worked with (observing confidentiality unless the clients have agreed that you can refer to them). By referring to clients conversationally, you communicate that you have experience with different organizations without having to reel off a list of big names. Stories bring some reality, humour and emotion into the process, and emotion engages people.

As an example, I was invited to pitch for a coaching programme in an engineering company in the far north of England. Most of the employees were men. I am a female business owner of a certain age, and I am from the south of England with all that goes with that in terms of the way I present myself. I could tell when I arrived that the people interviewing me had concerns about a mismatch. They questioned me about whether I had ever worked in this sort of environment before and how I thought coaching would be received in a place like this. I answered their questions by telling them about a similar organization where I had delivered coach training, which was not too far away from them. I told them that on the first day the participants had sat staring at me with their arms folded and had bandied around the phrase 'pink and fluffy' a few times. At the end of the day I just asked them to try what they had learned for themselves – at home, with their families and in the workplace. I suggested that if they found it did not work we would rethink the programme the next time we met. They came back for the second day of the programme three weeks later. The first thing I noticed was that most of them did not have their workbooks with them and I read this as a bad sign. However, when the workshop started I learned that they had lent their workbooks to their colleagues so that they could learn some of the techniques for themselves. All the participants admitted that they had been sceptical, but they had tried the coaching approaches and found them to work so powerfully that they wanted to share them with everyone they knew. Telling a true story, with enthusiasm and passion, was a far better response than trying to justify why I felt I was the right person for the job.

Beware of using too much coaching jargon. When we are well versed in a subject, it is easy to forget that not everybody else is familiar with it. We discount our coaching knowledge and expertise if we think that everybody knows it. Your GP, dentist or lawyer is unlikely to use scientific or technical terms when speaking to you. They use language that you will understand. So take a leaf from the books of other professionals and do not assume that everyone knows what the GROW model is or the Wheel of Life, and choose your language carefully when talking to prospective clients. You can inadvertently make clients feel bewildered or undermined because they are not familiar with these terms.

Be memorable (in a good way)

Organizations will usually arrive at a shortlist of three or four coaching providers, seeing each on the same day in a series of meetings. It's likely that most of the coaches will be saying similar things and the day can become repetitive for the panel doing the interviews. My colleague and I once had the 4 p.m. slot on a Friday afternoon for just such a meeting. When we signed in the visitor's book at reception, we saw the names of the five other companies that had already been there that day. When we walked in to face the panel, we saw eight exhausted people. I could almost read their minds: 'Please, no more PowerPoint.' We needed to change the atmosphere in the room so at the last minute we ditched our slide show and we coached the group instead. They livened up and we ended up laughing together – and we won the work. Instead of pressing on with our carefully planned presentation, we had behaved like coaches, responding to what we observed in the other people and spontaneously adjusting to the mood. Because of this, they saw our capacity to coach people to a more resourceful place. Behave like a coach when you are selling coaching or pitching for work. That means getting yourself, your agenda and your ego out of the way and concentrating on what the client wants.

Be true to yourself

Remember that pitching is a two-way process. By the time you have got through to the final round of interviews, you may decide that the work is not for you after all. My company has walked away from a few opportunities because we genuinely did not feel we were the right providers. We are also scrupulously honest with ourselves and the client organization about whether what we are asked to do is within our sphere of expertise.

It is important to have your own defined limits of what is acceptable to you in order to meet your own standards and values. For certain types of coaching workshops, my organization does not deliver single days of training. We have learned through experience that two separate days, with time for workplace practice in between, is more effective in embedding the learning. When we explain our reasons for this decision, we are demonstrating credibility, experience and knowledge as well as our integrity about the process.

Finally, do not try to be what you imagine a salesperson to be. Just be yourself. Do not learn a script and do not push to 'close the sale'. This approach does not work in a coaching context. Instead look forward to staying in touch with the organization and make the offer of further conversations if needed.

Coaching Exercises

Reflective questions about selling

What experiences have you had of selling yourself and your services? What were the most and least successful occasions, as you experienced them? What made the difference?

When you were successful, were you better prepared? Did you experience a different level of commitment to a successful outcome? How confident did you feel about your ability to do this particular work? How confident were you feeling generally? What support did you have to help you achieve a successful outcome?

When you were less successful, what tripped you up? How could you have avoided those obstacles? What could you do in future to make success more likely?

Dream board members exercise

Set some time aside to do this exercise. You may want to close your eyes and visualize or simply sit with pen and paper and think. Choose the way that works for you.

Put together your ideal board of directors. There are no limits to this exercise. You can choose real people, fictional characters, famous people from history. In fact, they don't even have to be people – you could have animals, cartoon characters or anyone else who comes to mind.

As you choose each person, make a note of what qualities and strengths they would bring to your business and any other reasons you have chosen them. Imagine them all together, in support of you, and think how powerful you would feel. You can even create an image to remind you of your dream board members.

When you are subsequently faced with a pitch, a proposal or a sales challenge, you can call to mind one or two of the board members who you think would deal with this challenge well: think what they would do or say to you.

Suggested Further Reading

Chandler, S. and Litvin, R. (2013) *The Prosperous Coach: Increase Income and Impact for You and Your Clients*. Anna Maria, FL: Maurice Bassett.

Oade, A. (2008) *Starting and Running a Coaching Business: The Complete Guide to Setting Up and Managing a Coaching Practice*. Oxford: How To Books Ltd.

Rogers, J. (2016) *Coaching Skills: The Definitive Guide to Being a Coach*, 4th edn. Maidenhead: Open University Press.

5 Managing Client Boundaries

Boundaries play a key role in coaching sessions and in building an effective coaching relationship. Clear boundaries build trust and show a respect for the confidential and personal nature of the coaching relationship. They also give the client a sense of understanding, certainty and respect. During your coach training you will have learned about building a coaching relationship, but having to do it for the first time with a paying client can still be a daunting process. This chapter will provide answers to some of the questions I am frequently asked by newly qualified coaches.

Your First Client

When you are training to be a coach, you generally practise your coaching skills on fellow students. They are all familiar with coaching and understand the unstated rules of such friendly practice. Even if you have been working with volunteer clients during your training, they are probably friends, contacts or colleagues who are keen to help you improve your competence and experience as a coach. They understand that you are still in training and they manage their expectations accordingly.

Once you have secured your first paying client, you must put into practice all you have learned about establishing trust and intimacy and creating a safe, supportive environment that produces ongoing mutual respect and trust. All sorts of concerns can spring to mind as the months of practice and theory become a reality. For example, coaches often worry that they won't like their clients and wonder what they would do if this happened. Other coaches want to understand how they can put aside their judgements. They question whether it is ever possible to maintain an attitude of unconditional positive regard.

Newly trained coaches working with clients for the first time often ask these questions:

- How much should I disclose about myself and my own life to my clients?
- What do I do if my client cries? Should I touch them on the arm? Offer them time out? Cry with them?

- Can you ever become friends with a client?
- When are you ever off-duty as a coach?
- How do I manage myself if my client reminds me of someone I know and don't like?

How Much Self-Disclosure is Appropriate?

Case Study 5.1: Rachel

Rachel is a new coach who is warm, encouraging and supportive. She has always had the ability to make people feel good about themselves and that is one of the reasons she decided to train as a coach. She enjoys helping people and knowing that she has made a difference to their lives. She learned on her coach training course that she is comfortable championing and praising her clients, but that she struggles to be challenging. Rachel has a wide network of personal and professional contacts and has used her network to find coaching clients. Just six months after starting her business, she has ten regular coaching clients. However, she is struggling to maintain professional boundaries with some of her female clients. She gets along so well with some of them that they now greet one another with a hug and a kiss when they arrive for their coaching sessions. A couple of them have invited her to meet them outside the coaching sessions for a coffee or a glass of wine. Rachel is aware that she has probably shared too much of herself already and the coaching sessions are beginning to feel like the type of conversations she has with her friends.

Recently a client was in tears in a coaching session and Rachel leapt out of her chair and gave her a hug. It was immediately apparent that this gesture was not well received by the client and Rachel has been worrying about having encroached on the client's personal boundaries. Another client mentioned to Rachel that she had experienced a miscarriage. Rachel had also experienced a miscarriage and shared that information. As she told her story, Rachel could see from the look on her client's face that she was not at all interested and Rachel felt that the coaching relationship was damaged by this self-disclosure.

Rachel is keen to put some clearer professional boundaries in place, but old habits die hard for her and she is not sure how to change her behaviour with her existing clients.

Being a warm, caring person who is comfortable with their own emotions is an asset to you when you are a coach. It enables you to build rapport easily and model being at ease with emotions. It also means that you provide an authentic experience of human interaction in the coaching session, rather than a formal or distant relationship. Possibly, like Rachel in Case Study 5.1, your outgoing personality will also help you to access a wide network of contacts to generate coaching clients. Self-disclosure from the coach can be helpful to clients but how do you know when, what and how much to disclose? How do you assess the benefit or downside to your client of your self-disclosure? Coaching is not therapy, but coaches have drawn extensively on therapeutic models during the evolution of coaching practice, particularly in relation to the coaching alliance or relationship.

In the early days of psychotherapy, self-disclosure by therapists was entirely off limits. Freud believed that the therapist should be impenetrable to the patient and that the therapist's role was to reflect back only what the patient gave him. He argued that this approach allowed the client to project their thoughts and feelings onto the blank screen of the therapist. This enabled the therapist to experience the client's assumptions and projections about themselves and other people. Freud believed that the blank screen approach would create in the client a state of 'optimal frustration', which would uncover the client's ego defences. If, for example, the client believed that nobody was to be trusted, they would not trust the therapist. If, however, the therapist reassured the client and presented himself as a kind, caring and trustworthy person, the client would not be able to work through such deep-seated beliefs and assumptions in the same dynamic way. Another reason for lack of self-disclosure by psychodynamic therapists was to ensure that the entire therapeutic hour was dedicated to the client and none of it to the therapist. How Freud and his contemporaries interacted with their clients in practice is a separate question, but, theoretically at least, self-disclosure was not permitted.

Over time the restrictions on self-disclosure in the helping and talking professions loosened. In the 1960s and 1970s proponents of the humanistic, person-centred approach to counselling argued that self-disclosure could be therapeutic and helpful to the client. Humanistic therapists suggested that if practitioners demonstrated their vulnerability and revealed the unresolved issues in their own lives, clients would come to accept that everyone has failings, and their own situation would come to seem more normal. Self-help groups emerged around the same time, working on the basis of self-disclosure by group members and the group leader. This mutual self-disclosure provided some normalization for the group members and enabled them to learn that they were not alone in their feelings or situations.

Self-disclosure can be a deliberate choice by the coach (see Case Study 5.2), and it can take two different forms. Deliberate self-disclosure often happens in the contracting or chemistry conversation with a client when you give some information about yourself: qualifications, previous career experience, areas of interest for coaching and possibly personal circumstances. Another form of deliberate self-disclosure can be sharing your thoughts and feelings about something the client is saying or something that has happened in the session: 'I really admire the way you deal with difficulties' or 'I couldn't help feeling outraged on your behalf when you told me that story'. You could also decide to share an experience you have had which is similar to your client's experience: 'I'm not surprised you felt anxious when you were speaking at a conference of 100 delegates. I do a lot of public speaking and I still feel some nerves every time I walk onto the stage.' You can use deliberate self-disclosure to change a client's perception of themselves: 'You often refer to yourself as a nervous person. I would like to observe that I don't experience you as a nervous person. On the contrary, I always think you look calm and at ease with yourself.'

Self-disclosure can also be prompted by the client asking you a direct question: 'Where do you live?', 'Do you have children?', 'How did you feel when you first started your own business?' Clients can sometimes become curious about you and your life. I know one client who experienced the tragic death of her young child and wanted to know whether her coach was a mother too, in the belief that she would have a better understanding of her grief if she was a parent herself. You will need to make a judgement about how to deal with these direct enquiries into your life. You can ask your client gently, 'What is important to you about knowing that?' or you can simply answer the question succinctly and then move your focus back to your client. You will need to decide whether your response will enhance trust, intimacy and rapport in the coaching relationship.

Unplanned self-disclosure can occur in different ways too. Your accent and how you present yourself physically will give information about you to your client. If you work from a home office, your surroundings will give away clues to you and your life, and this is something you should be aware of. You can read more about this in Chapter 6. Your social media profile is also something you need to consider in terms of how much you allow clients to know about you.

You might find yourself, spontaneously and without intention, sharing your experiences, stories or personal circumstances with your client in the way you would with a friend: 'Oh, yes, I love the Greek islands too. I have been going there for years. Where do you stay when you go there?' Unless this type of self-disclosure is made for the client's benefit or the benefit of the coaching relationship, it is more likely to be about meeting your own needs. You can usually see immediately in your client's body language when your self-disclosure has not been welcomed. From time to time you might want to review with your client how much your self-disclosure has benefited them in their coaching sessions.

Occasionally you may be hooked into reliving painful memories of your own if your client's situation reminds you of something in your life. This can lead to unplanned self-disclosure of a different kind. If, in response to a client discussing a bereavement, you were to say, 'I remember when my mother died – it was a traumatic time for me and I still miss her terribly', it could throw the coaching relationship out of kilter. It might even produce a role reversal, with the client feeling the need to take care of you.

Planned and intentional self-disclosure should always be for your client's benefit. If you find yourself making disclosures about yourself in an unplanned way, you will need to discuss this in supervision and explore what need this is serving for you.

> **Case Study 5.2: Babs**
>
> Babs had always been a gregarious person, who described herself as an 'open book'. She decided to become a coach because her own life had been full of trials and tribulations and she wanted to be able to coach others who were going through difficult times. She had never been entirely convinced about the idea that clients will find their own answers if you create the right conditions for them. Babs' coaching sessions always included her sharing her 'wisdom' and life experiences. Sometimes she noticed her clients glaze over when she was talking about herself. One day, a client wrote to Babs to say that she no longer wanted to work with her. The client had recently been given a coach at work and for the first time had experienced a coach who provided an uninterrupted thinking space, which she had found far more beneficial than the work she had done with Babs. Babs was shocked and disappointed to have been dismissed by a client. She reflected on what she should do and concluded that she wanted to bring her story and her experiences to her coaching practice. Babs didn't change her approach but did change her marketing and her contracting with clients so that they were very clear about what they would be getting.

How Do I Respond if My Client Cries in a Coaching Session?

It is not at all unusual for clients to cry in coaching sessions. Just coming to the session and feeling free to talk can release emotions. Clients cry for many reasons: tears can express joy, as well as sorrow, frustration and anger. Your role is to show your client that you are comfortable with emotions, theirs and your own. This means being still, waiting, listening, demonstrating warmth and care and continuing to provide a safe space. It does not mean looking alarmed or asking them immediately if they want to stop the session, as this response can give the client a message that it is inappropriate to demonstrate high levels of emotion in a coaching session. Jumping up to hug them could be seen as infantilizing or rescuing and could be received as an invasion of their personal boundaries. If you begin to cry with your client, they could interpret this as meaning that their situation must be really desperate – or, on the other hand, that you are not capable of providing the safe space they need to explore their emotions to the full.

If the crying persists, ask your client gently what they would like to do and they will tell you. It is not up to you to decide what is best for them. You need to demonstrate your trust in their ability to manage themselves. If you feel the need to offer some physical gesture of care, such as taking their hand or putting an arm on their shoulder, always ask if this is something your client would welcome, even if you have already discussed physical space and touch in initial contracting conversations.

I Really Like My Client. Is it OK to Meet Them Socially and Become Friends with Them?

Other helping professions such as counselling and therapy have very clear ethical guidelines about relationships with clients. These state that becoming friends is not permitted. Even if you were to see your therapist, by chance, in a social setting, it is likely that they would not acknowledge you. The belief which underpins this guideline is that confidentiality is paramount, and any crossing of boundaries will affect the therapeutic alliance.

I draw on comparisons between coaching and therapy in this book because there are decades of research into the therapeutic relationship and, by comparison, still limited research about the client–coach relationship. There is no doubt that there are similarities between the two as they are both 'helping by talking' relationships. However, coaching differs from therapy in a number of ways, and one of those differences is that the guidelines about friendships with clients are not as clearly specified. The International Coach Federation's *Code of Ethics* (ICF 2015) warns specifically about avoiding romantic or sexual relationships with clients, but friendship with clients is not explicitly mentioned.

However, the Standards of Conduct in the ICF *Code of Ethics* include the following:

- 'I will seek to avoid conflicts between my interests and the interests of my clients.'
- 'I will not knowingly exploit any aspect of the coach–client relationship for my personal, professional or monetary advantage or benefit.'
- 'If I believe the client would be better served by another coach . . . I will encourage the client to make a change.'

Coaching and therapy typically arise from different kinds of need on the part of the client, and coaching can occur in a broader range of contexts. You may find yourself coaching someone you have known for a long time, such as a business contact, a colleague or even a friend. There is no explicit requirement to stop socializing with them once coaching begins. If you are working as an internal coach in an organization, it is likely that you will continue to interact regularly with your coaching clients – professionally and perhaps socially too. As it stands, coaches are left to make the ethical decision about whether or not they socialize with their clients. If you are thinking about coaching a friend or colleague, discussions about whether you continue to socialize with one another for the duration of your coaching relationship can be part of your initial contracting together.

If you coach a friend, you will both already have established patterns and expectations about your roles in your relationship. You will be used to reciprocity in your conversations, for example. If you enter a coaching relationship, this will completely change and your client will lead the agenda and the direction of the conversation. This could be a difficult transition for you both to make, particularly if you have well-practised ways of being together. Your shared personal history could prevent you from seeing your client with the fresh eyes and objectivity that coaching requires. It could also prevent your client from talking candidly with you for fear of adversely affecting the way you see them or harming your friendship.

If you regularly feel as though you could become friends with your clients, it is worth taking this pattern to your supervision sessions. What does it say about you, your professional boundaries and, perhaps, your own unmet needs? If once in a while you coach someone with whom you feel you have a strong connection and you think you would like to become friends with them, leave the discussion about becoming friends until the coaching is finished. If you do decide to socialize together later on, you should be aware that it will make it harder for you to resume a professional relationship with them if they want more coaching in the future. It will also be difficult not to fall into an informal coach/client relationship in which the other person is benefiting from your coaching skills without paying for them.

What if my client wants to be my friend?

Most coaches have highly developed listening skills along with rapport-building ability and a genuine interest in other people. These are some of the core skills of our trade. However, a professional coaching attitude can give some clients the mistaken impression that they just happen to have met someone with whom they really 'click'. They may believe that they have struck up a friendship. This tends to happen if the role of the coach has not been clearly explained in the contracting session, or if the client is lacking friendship or affection elsewhere in their life. It can be an indication of the phenomenon psychologists call 'transference', where the coach reminds the client of a significant person in their past to whom they had warm feelings and they are now transferring the same feelings to the coach. It can also happen if the coach does not achieve the right balance of intimacy in the coaching relationship because of an excessive need to be liked by others. This kind of coach overuses compliments and support for their clients to the point of flattery and is reluctant to challenge them. If a client thinks that you want to be their friend, they may initiate the idea of socializing together. You will need to consider carefully what has given rise to this suggestion and, if necessary, re-contract with your client about roles, responsibilities and expectations. You may also want to address this issue in your supervision sessions, particularly if it is a repeating pattern for you.

How to Be Off-Duty as a Coach

Case Study 5.3: John and Sandra

John and Sandra are a married couple who are both coaches. They mostly socialize with other coaches. Some of their coaching clients have become their friends and some of their old friends have now trained as coaches. John and Sandra are very clear that they can coach each other, coach their friends, be coached by their friends and maintain very clear boundaries between their personal relationships and their coaching relationships.

If John and Sandra have a coaching session at home, they mark out the time and space very clearly. They move into their home office, they set a time limit and they metaphorically put on their 'coaching hats'. When the session is over, they take off their 'coaching hats' and they agree never to discuss the content of the coaching sessions when they step back into their personal life. It works well for them, and they know that it requires robust contracting and high levels of trust.

During your coach training or when you are newly qualified, it can be difficult to refrain from coaching everyone you know, particularly when you are enthused by your new skills. Family and friends will probably let you know in no uncertain terms that you are no longer having two-way conversations and that you are behaving like their coach and not their friend. This compulsion to coach everyone you meet usually wears off quite quickly once you start coaching actual clients. It can happen the other way around too. For example, you may find yourself at a social occasion telling people what you do for a living, only to find them asking you for advice and support about their lives and careers.

Coaching is a professional relationship that needs to be formally contracted by both parties. It is your responsibility to ensure that you manage clear boundaries between your professional life and social life (see Case Study 5.3). There is an apocryphal story about a doctor at a drinks party who was approached by a fellow guest seeking advice on a medical issue. The doctor, tired of such situations and wanting to enjoy the party, asked the guest to take off his trousers there and then so he could examine him. It had the desired effect. The other guest beat a hasty retreat, leaving the doctor to enjoy his gin and tonic in peace.

What Do I Do if I Don't Like My Client?

Case Study 5.4: Bob

Bob has been coaching for nearly five years. He worked as a senior manager before becoming a coach and has gradually built up a successful coaching business, mostly coaching managers working in engineering. He also works as an associate coach for a large coaching company, which recently put him forward for a chemistry session with the CEO of a large organization. Bob had not coached anyone with such a senior role before and felt a bit intimidated by the client when they met. To Bob's surprise, the CEO selected Bob as his coach. In the chemistry session Bob had not felt at ease with the client and went against his instincts in accepting the offer of work. He wishes now that he had listened to his 'gut', but was led by his ego as he was flattered to have been chosen. They have had two coaching sessions and Bob is still feeling intimidated by his client. He says that he feels paralysed by fear in the sessions and does not feel that he is giving his client his best service. Bob has discussed the situation with his coaching supervisor and realizes that the client reminds Bob of his father, who was an intimidating presence in Bob's life. Bob's response of 'freezing' with his client is exactly what he used to do with his father. Bob is seriously considering pulling out of the coaching. However, he knows that this will reflect badly on him as an associate and he does not want to let the company down.

What do you do if, despite your best efforts to suspend your judgement, you still find it difficult to work with a client because you don't like them? This question arises from time to time in supervision sessions. Of course, you do not need to actively like all your clients but you do need to have a positive regard for them as fellow human beings. It is inevitable that you will have favourite clients whom you look forward to seeing more than others. However, if your feelings towards your client, whether positive or negative, are getting in the way of your ability to work with them, you will need to address this.

Sometimes a negative response to your client can be caused by *countertransference*. This is a psychological term for what happens when a coach brings into the coaching sessions their own feelings or life experiences to the extent that they lose their professional objectivity.

An example of countertransference would be that a client reminds you of someone from your past and elicits in you the same response as you had to that person. Or you might over-identify with your client because you have similar backgrounds, experiences or personalities.

It could also be that the client is eliciting from you the same emotional response that they elicit from others. It is important to ask yourself the question, 'Am I feeling what others are feeling in response to my client and, if so, does this information give me an insight into the effect my client has on people generally?' As a coach, you need to be attentive to your feelings about your client. Your feelings give you valuable information for you to reflect on and discuss with your supervisor. With supervision, support and reflection it is often possible to develop an understanding of what is happening in the relationship between you and your client and to use this information to deepen the coaching relationship.

Sometimes, it is helpful to discuss your feelings openly with a client. I had one client who was a beautiful and playful young woman who was always desperately late for our sessions. Finally, she would arrive bearing cupcakes and flowers for me and apologizing profusely. I noticed that she stood with her feet pointing inwards, and often put her finger on her mouth and made a comic book sad face. She looked like a cute but naughty child and I did not challenge her on her lateness.

Having discussed this case with my supervisor, I realized that I was feeling parental and indulgent. She charmed me with her childlike behaviour and I lost all my ability to behave in a professional way. It took courage, but I explained this to her in one of our sessions. As we discussed it, we uncovered that this was a behaviour she adopted to get her own way at work and in personal relationships. It was clear that, while it worked for her in the short term, it was not a successful long-term strategy. She had used it successfully with her father for her entire life and mistakenly believed it would go on working with other people. For the rest of our time together, she worked towards developing an 'adult-to-adult' communication style and taking personal responsibility for her actions.

There may be times when you simply cannot overcome your feelings about a client and you know that you are not giving the client an effective service. If this is the case, the best course of action is probably to end the coaching assignment. Making the decision to end an assignment is a big step and you will need support from your supervisor to plan exactly how you are going to do it. The most important outcome is for the client to understand that the problem or difficulty lies with you, thereby leaving the client's self-esteem intact.

I was once seeing a therapist, who told me she could no longer work with me because she said I was very 'convincing' and therefore she believed everything I told her, and she had lost objectivity. It really shook me, and I started to doubt my reasons for being warm and friendly and questioned my authenticity. It took me a few months' work with another therapist to deal with the impact of this rejection. While it can be valuable in coaching sessions to discuss countertransference, it is not helpful to introduce this suddenly as a reason for ending the coaching assignment. I would simply suggest letting the client know that you do not think you are the best person to give them the service they need. If you can support them by referring them to another coach, this will help to ease their transition. You will need to deal with an ending of this kind with the utmost care and integrity. Even so, the possibility remains that it could be a real setback for your client and could also have an impact on your reputation.

In Case Study 5.4, Bob was working as an associate for a larger company when he encountered a client who created feelings of discomfort in him. If you ever find yourself in a similar situation, it is important to communicate with the company for whom you are delivering this coaching work as soon as possible. They may be able to give you some support or supervision. Equally, they will probably have an existing relationship with the client organization and may be able to negotiate your withdrawal from the process and provide a replacement coach. Situations in which coaches do not like their clients should be rare. If this is something that happens regularly for you, it should alert you to the need for more supervision, personal coaching or some other means of developing a greater understanding of yourself.

Coaching Exercises

Changing places with your client

Imagine changing places with your client and being coached by you. Picture sitting opposite you, as coach.

Then ask yourself, from the perspective of being your client, the following questions:

- How does it feel to be coached by this person?
- How well do they balance support and challenge in my sessions?
- How far do I believe them when they give me positive feedback?
- How clear are their boundaries about time, money, the coaching relationship, confidentiality?
- How much do they explicitly tell me about themselves? How useful is this to me?
- How much do they implicitly tell me about themselves (via their appearance, their voice, their behaviours, their surroundings)?
- What aspects of them would I like to be different?
- What are their strengths as a coach?
- What are their areas for development as a coach?

Come back to being yourself and reflect on what you have learned from that exercise. What can you do to create an even more professional and safe space for your clients?

Reflective practice on your response to clients

Think about a client you look forward to seeing and with whom you really 'click', and another client with whom you find it difficult to build rapport. For each of these two clients ask yourself the following questions:

- Who does this client remind me of?
- How do I feel before this client arrives for their coaching session?
- What is my inner dialogue about this client?
- If I were to allow my judgements about this client to surface, what would they be?
- What do I avoid with this client?
- What do I notice about myself and my client when we meet? What happens between us?
- What metaphor can I find for the relationship I have with this client? (In this chapter I gave an example about my client who behaved like a naughty child, so my metaphor for our relationship would be that I was an overindulgent mother and she was my spoilt child. A powerful executive coach I know describes his coaching relationship with a CEO as 'two lions in a den'.)

Suggested Further Reading

Egan, G. (2001) *The Skilled Helper: A Problem-Management Approach to Helping*, 4th edn. Pacific Grove, CA: Brooks/Cole Publishing Company.

Hay, J. (2007) *Reflective Practice and Supervision for Coaches*. Maidenhead: Open University Press.

Sandler, C. (2011) *Executive Coaching: A Psychodynamic Approach*. Maidenhead: Open University Press.

6 Boundaries of Time and Place

Coaching should be a place of sanctuary for clients – a safe space where they can think for themselves in the presence of a skilled coach. A first step towards creating this safe space is to consider the boundaries of time and place. Paying attention to the physical space in which you meet your clients is an essential part of being a coach and time management is key in all coaching, wherever it takes place. This chapter will explore the psychological aspects of time and place and give you some more information on why they are important to coach and client equally.

It is easy to rush the practical formalities of the coaching session, or overlook them altogether, disregarding the 'boring' ethical rules, because you want to get on with the 'real business' of coaching and start using all the wonderful tools and techniques you have learned. However, establishing the coaching relationship is very much the 'real business' of coaching. Setting clear boundaries of time and place creates a secure foundation for the coaching relationship. Most coaches find themselves regularly having to make decisions about time and other boundary issues:

- Should I see coaching clients in my own home?
- My client has asked me to accompany them to a meeting at their workplace. Should I go?
- Is it OK to coach my client in a public space, like a hotel lobby or a coffee shop?
- My coaching sessions often run over time – is this OK?
- What do I do if the client is in a state of high emotion at the end of the session – should I extend the session to allow the client to compose themself?
- My client is always late for the session and I am not sure whether I should challenge this lateness.

Good contracting is key in coaching, and all logistical details about time and space should be covered in the initial coaching contract (see Chapter 4, 'Contracting, Pitching and Client Meetings'). However, sometimes coaches are in a hurry to get on with the coaching itself and omit the finer details in their contracting sessions. This is understandable if there is also a written contract, but not all coaches provide written contracts. Even with a contract in place, you may still be uncertain about whether it is acceptable for you to transgress boundaries in extraordinary circumstances.

Where Should I Meet Clients?

Case Study 6.1: Chris

Chris is a newly qualified coach. He took redundancy from his HR role in a national retail organization and invested his savings in a professional coach training programme. Chris was fired up about his new career direction at the end of his coach training course, but he is currently finding it hard to adjust to self-employment. He did not realize how much he would miss the camaraderie of a large team and the resources provided by a large organization. He has not been used to having to do everything himself – marketing, writing his website, finding clients and touting for coaching assignments. He has not earned much money in his first few months of trading.

Chris has been concerned about where coaching sessions should take place. He does not have a designated office space in his home and is keen to coach clients somewhere away from their work environment, both to ensure confidentiality and to provide them with a neutral thinking space. So far, Chris has been meeting clients in hotel lobbies or coffee shops but has generally found the experience to be unsatisfactory. Noise levels and lack of privacy have meant that he has been unable to practise all the dynamic listening skills and the creative coaching techniques that he learned during his training. He reported that one of his clients had become highly emotional during a recent coaching session in a crowded hotel lobby and it had been an uncomfortable experience for both of them. Chris has looked into the cost of hiring private meeting rooms but feels they are outside his budget. He would not make any money at all from his coaching work if he continued to charge the same fees for coaching. He has considered increasing his fees to incorporate the meeting room costs but, as a new coach who is struggling to get business anyway, he does not feel that this is a realistic solution.

Where coaching sessions should take place has become a topic of lively debate in the coaching world. There is virtually universal agreement that the quality of the relationship between coach and client is the primary factor in determining the success of a coaching intervention. There is also a generally accepted assumption that the ideal conditions for this relationship to develop involve one-to-one meetings in a safe, comfortable space, removed from the distractions of everyday life and work.

But how does a freelance coach with limited resources, like Chris in Case Study 6.1, fund a private coaching room? Or how can the manager of a remote team, spread across two continents, create this safe environment? Internal coaches in organizations often have to fight to find suitable meeting rooms and end up coaching in public areas. Even if they do find a meeting room, it is often not genuinely private, and confidentiality can easily be compromised.

In her book *Time to Think*, Nancy Kline (1999: 84–6) recommends 'creating a physical environment that says to people, "You matter"'. Research in environmental psychology has provided evidence to support our instinctive knowledge that our physical environment does have a direct impact on our thoughts, feelings and behaviours. Feeling a sense of ease, safety and security about our surroundings enables us to be more relaxed and therefore to be more open to reflection and learning. Our clients need to feel safe and secure in the coaching 'place' so that they can speak honestly and without fear of being overheard.

In an ideal world, every coach would have their own private coaching rooms, comfortably furnished and fully equipped with everything that might be needed for coaching sessions, but that is not the reality for most coaches. So, until you can create your own ideal coaching room, here are some ways to make the physical environment of the coaching session work better for you and your client. There is often no perfect solution, but it is worth taking time to consider the advantages, disadvantages and limitations of each of the options.

Your home

Case Study 6.2: Toni

Toni had a summerhouse in her garden which she used as a coaching room. It was peaceful, away from the house, heated in winter and beautifully furnished. Most of her clients loved being coached in the garden sanctuary Toni had created. Toni was proud of her coaching room and felt she had successfully solved the problem of 'where to coach', and the bonus was not having to travel to work.

Then a new client told Toni that she felt very uneasy about the venue. She said she felt 'catapulted' into Toni's world from the moment she arrived at the house. She had to walk through the garden, which gave so many clues about Toni's personal life: washing on the line, children's toys on the lawn and two cats which ran to greet the client and – to her horror – rubbed up against her legs. Sometimes she was able to see people in the house and wondered who they were and if they knew all about her and why she was having coaching. Even Toni's carefully styled room betrayed too many aspects of Toni. Although this was a one-off piece of feedback, Toni wondered whether other clients felt the same way but did not feel able to say so. She continued working from her summerhouse but removed many of the personal items, and in future made sure that there was no washing on the line on the days she had coaching clients.

Working from a designated space in your own home presents both coach and client with particular challenges. Seeing clients in your home inevitably blurs the boundaries between your personal and professional life. I recall, early in my own career, a client coming to my home for a coaching session. He got out of his car, looked up at my house and said, 'No wonder you are charging me so much if you need to pay the mortgage on this.' Another client walked through the entrance hall, picked up some photographs of my children from the hall table and began asking me questions about my family life.

If you are working from home, robust contracting with your client about the boundaries is essential and you will also need to have boundary-setting conversations with your family. If you are going to coach at home, the ideal arrangement would be to have a designated area for coaching, separate from the rest of the home, with its own private entrance and a bathroom for client use only (see Case Study 6.2).

There are two advantages, for both coach and client, of having a home office: it reduces the overheads and it allows you to create a more comfortable and homely space than an impersonal meeting room.

But there are also some obvious disadvantages. Even if the coach is able to limit the presence of personal items such as family photographs, unintentional self-disclosure by the coach via non-verbal signals is inevitable, raising confidentiality and privacy issues for both client and coach. The potential presence of the coach's family members increases the possibility of interruptions or of confidential coaching conversations being inadvertently overheard. Issues may arise concerning access to other parts of the coach's home or use of other facilities. And, because it exposes the coach to the risk of liability in the case of accidents, public liability insurance will be necessary. Other considerations include how centrally you live, whether there is parking available and public transport links.

The client's workplace

Coaching frequently takes place in the workplace. This has some obvious attractions for organizations and for busy clients. It is cheap and time-efficient. If you attend the workplace, you are on hand, if required, for briefing and three-way meetings with the coachee's line manager or sponsor where such meetings are part of the contracted programme.

There are some practical concerns. Clients will often find it very difficult to switch off from the demands and stresses of the office. Emails will be accumulating on their screens and phones and their day's to-do list will be neglected while they sit with the coach in a meeting room. There is also the possibility of interruptions. There may be no way of keeping it from other employees that the client is being coached, and it may be difficult to maintain the feeling of confidentiality, privacy or safety. It may be harder for the client to feel confident that the coach is truly independent of the organization and not perhaps on the side of the employer. In large organizations, there is also the problem of what I now call the 'meeting room space race'. It happens frequently that my corporate clients book a meeting room for their coaching session with me but when we get there, a group of people has already seized the empty room for a meeting of their own; we have to ask them to leave and convince them that we had pre-booked the room, before we can start on the coaching. Sometimes, people open the door mid-coaching session to see if the room is free, which is not ideal in terms of confidentiality or flow of the session. At other times, the rooms are double-booked. Often meeting rooms are glass-fronted and I have sometimes noticed my clients looking anxiously over their shoulders, worrying about confidentiality, as colleagues walk past the room. The glass doors also mean I need to be mindful of anything I write up on flip charts in the coaching session, as they are visible to passers-by.

The major potential downsides to coaching in the workplace are psychological. The workplace is, after all, not generally the employee's own place. Being coached at work may make it much more difficult for the client to detach themselves from their habitual patterns of thought and feeling than if the meeting took place in a neutral space. This is particularly likely to be a problem if the client is experiencing stress or discomfort at work, which they may be if the client's manager or employer has requested a coaching intervention or if the coaching relates to work issues.

If you are coaching in your client's workplace, how can you limit the potential disadvantages and help your client to get the best out of your coaching sessions? Address the practical issues. Rearrange the furniture so that it does not look like a typical office or meeting room. Agree that mobile phones will be switched off. Put up a 'do not disturb' sign if that would help. Openly acknowledge the potential limitations and constraints of being in their workplace and discuss with your client how comfortable they feel about privacy and self-disclosure in this environment. Begin each session with a brief and light-hearted ritual in which the client lets go of all work-related thoughts and behaviours. Putting aside the technology can be part of the ritual. Sometimes your client might like to take off their jacket or shoes. Between you, you might find a piece of music that helps them to shift their mental and emotional state. Often some simple physical movement will help to shake off the work state and get ready for coaching.

Private meeting rooms

There is no doubt that a safe, private and confidential space will create the ideal conditions for coaching to take place and provide an environment which allows full scope for movement, emotion, creativity and freedom of expression. This sort of dedicated space really does give your clients the message that they matter and that this work is important. Admittedly this option comes at a price, but it need not necessarily be a high one. An internet search throws up meeting rooms around the UK which can be rented for as little as £10 an hour. Sometimes gyms, health clubs or spas have small meeting rooms which they rent out by the hour, as do church halls, hotels, social clubs and business centres. Some coaches build the cost of room hire into the fee for the coaching session. I know a number of coaches who barter their services in exchange for meeting rooms; one coach runs a monthly coaching workshop for members of a health club in exchange for free use of a meeting room.

Coaching out of doors

You could consider coaching your client while you walk together outdoors. Your client will get the immediate benefits of fresh air and space and freedom in which to focus on their thoughts, away from their usual environment, and the bonus of a bit of exercise. And it doesn't cost anything. You don't need to live in an area of beautiful countryside or even near a park. You can walk and coach just as effectively in an urban landscape.

Coaching while walking has some powerful effects. For example, physical mobility often increases mobility in our thinking. It presents an ideal opportunity for you to work with your client at the level of metaphors and symbols by using the sights, sounds, sensations and even the smells around you as you walk together. The meaning a client unconsciously attaches to things can provide coach and client with valuable insights. As you walk, ask your client to let you know if they are noticing anything particular in the landscape. If they notice something, ask them to talk about what has caught their attention. Through coaching questions, invite the client to consider whether it might have any relevance to any aspect of their current situation. Maybe something of significance will surface, maybe it won't. If it doesn't, don't linger. Just walk on and ask the client to continue noticing what they notice. I was once coaching a woman who was going through a relationship break-up. Until we walked together she had chosen not to speak to me about her relationship during coaching sessions but wanted to focus on work-related issues. She had assured me that she had dealt with the relationship break-up and was keen to move on with planning her life. While we were walking together, her attention was repeatedly drawn to a telegraph wire where one lone sparrow sat some distance away from a group of other birds. Through this unconscious metaphor and her instinctive empathy with the sparrow she was able to use the session to explore for the first time her feelings of isolation, loneliness and loss about the end of her relationship.

Some clients will find walking alongside you a relief from the intensity of direct eye contact while sitting face to face. They may find themselves able to speak to you more freely as you walk companionably alongside one another. Simply changing how coach and client are physically positioned in relation to one another in this way can enhance the partnering aspect of the client/coach relationship. Coaching while walking can work particularly well for clients who are desk-bound and stressed at work. It takes them into an entirely different environment, which can free their thinking and give them a new perspective, literally and metaphorically.

Case Study 6.3: Owen

Owen is a coach who lives in one of the UK's historic cities. He is proud of his city and he enjoys its museums, parks and places of cultural interest. Owen had the idea of walking and coaching around the city in the summer and meeting his clients for coaching in art galleries, museums and other public buildings on cold or rainy days. What started as a novel idea has become the only way in which Owen coaches, and something which differentiates him from other coaches. He is now a sought-after coach because of his different approach. Owen believes this way of working has added depth and creativity to his coaching sessions. Clients are able to choose statues and pieces of art as metaphors to describe their feelings or hopes and dreams. Many clients take photographs throughout their coaching sessions as visual reminders. Owen believes that being exposed to art, history, landscape and culture allows his clients to access emotions more readily. From his point of view, Owen says he never has to make notes and can always recall exactly what happened in every coaching session because of the sensory nature of the coaching session.

There are a few things to consider if, like Owen in Case Study 6.3, you are planning to coach in places of interest. You will, of course, need to check opening and closing times and entry fees. As these types of visit are activities you would normally do with friends or family, you will have to maintain clear boundaries and a focus and structure to the session to differentiate the experience from a social activity.

Remember that places of beauty are still public places, and that confidentiality can be compromised because there will be other people around you. If you are working in your home town, you and your client may also risk bumping into friends and you will have to agree with your client in advance how you will manage these encounters.

Coffee shops or hotel lobbies

If clients are to get the best from a coaching session, external distractions and stressors need to be minimized. The attention of the client or the coach can easily be broken by noise or visual distractions. If meeting in a coffee shop or hotel lobby is your only option, you need to accept that you are not providing an ideal environment (although some coaches find it works well – see Case Study 6.4). You may be able to select a place that does not have a large screen television showing 24-hour news or sport, or music blaring out of speakers in every corner of the room, but it is harder to avoid other people's noisy conversations. Even if you arrive early and find a quiet corner, you cannot guarantee that it will stay quiet. Consider how you would feel if you met your GP, lawyer or financial advisor in a noisy public space. Are you really giving your client the care and respect they deserve by meeting them here? If you do decide to meet a client in a public space, acknowledge to them before you start that there are likely to be distractions and ask them at the end of the session how the venue worked for them. If you believe that the coaching session is likely to be emotionally charged, you probably need to find an alternative venue, for that particular session at least.

Case Study 6.4: Kiran

Kiran has always met his clients in hotel lobbies. He has never paid for room hire and is confident that his clients are happy with the location. He thinks that the coaching space is created between the client and the coach and is not dependent on the physical surroundings. Once the coaching session starts, Kiran says any outside noises fade away and he and his client are in a coaching 'bubble'. Kiran's clients have laughed and cried, and he has used all kinds of creative coaching techniques in his sessions without anyone taking any notice. Kiran likes the fact that the hotels are anonymous places and the decor is a blank slate, which doesn't distract from the coaching work.

Telephone, video-conferencing or online coaching

Advances and improvements in technology have made coaching at distance a favoured way of working with clients for many coaches. Distance coaching gives coaches the opportunity to work with clients all over the world and it is time- and cost-effective, which is an advantage for organizations, coaches and clients alike. If you are coaching via computer, using a video-conferencing platform such as Skype or Zoom, contract clearly with your client about how this will work, paying particular attention to how you will manage the progress and timing of coaching sessions. If you are coaching by phone, ask the client how they would like you to signal that you are listening, and how they would like to signal to you when they have finished speaking.

Build in preparation and reflection time for yourself both before and after the session. Make sure you have any notes or resources to hand. Master the technology so that the technological process is seamless for you and your client. Create a virtual place which says to your client, 'You matter'. You could always play the same piece of music at the start of a phone or Skype session or begin each session with the same spoken introduction. Ensure that no mobiles or landlines can ring, and that any people who may be around while you are coaching do not intrude. If possible, sit in the same place each time and ensure that the client sees the same background view – take care that the background view is neutral and not distracting for the client.

Have confidence that creative and transformational coaching techniques can work for your client even when you are not with them in person. If you are going to use a creative approach in a session, it may be useful to alert your client to any resources they will need with them before the session starts, for example, paper and coloured pens, and any other props that you think you might need, even modelling dough such as Play-Doh. If you have any coaching exercises you would like your client to use, email copies of the materials to them in advance so that they can print them out ready for your session. Trust in your client's ability to manage their own emotional state and in your ability to support their development without being physically present.

Managing Time Boundaries

Case Study 6.5: Anna

Anna is a newly qualified coach who is keen to prove herself in her new career. She finds that her coaching sessions regularly run over time. On balance, Anna feels that this is justified and it is a legitimate response to her clients' needs. Anna says:

> I often find that we are just beginning to get somewhere really important at the end of the session and it seems wrong to stop the session at the scheduled time. It also feels abrupt and callous to end the session at a moment when my client is in crisis or high emotion. I'm just not sure whether I should extend the session to allow the client to continue to express themselves or whether I should just acknowledge what the client has said, end the session at the agreed time and ensure that I pick up the topic the next time we meet.

The importance of good beginnings and endings

Time boundaries play a key role in coaching sessions (see Case Study 6.5). There are obvious practical advantages to managing time well. How well you manage time while coaching will also give your clients a clear message about your general management of boundaries. If you do not respect time boundaries, your client will wonder, consciously or unconsciously, whether you approach other important boundaries in the same way. They may fear that you may have the same loose boundaries around issues such as confidentiality or fees, which could undermine their trust in you. If you are careless about time boundaries, you are also communicating messages about how you value yourself, and thus how others should value you. What are you saying about yourself and about your value as a coach if you give your client more time than has been contracted and paid for?

Managing time for the benefit of your client is one of your responsibilities as a coach. It gives the session a clear framework and ensures a sense of safety. Having a clear beginning, middle and end for each session is an effective way of maintaining boundaries for your client. It is valuable to remind your client at the start of the session how long the session will last and to keep them informed during the session how much time is left. It is particularly important to signal in advance when the session is coming towards its end. This gives the client the opportunity to control how the time is used, and to manage their self-disclosure in the session.

Clients often come to coaching with an idea of what they want to discuss. However, it will often take time to build up the level of trust to a point where they feel able to let their guard down and talk about what is most important to them. They may think they are ready to share their deepest hopes, dreams and fears in the coaching session but unconsciously they will tend to protect themselves until they feel safe. This is why the beginnings and the ends of coaching sessions can be moments of particular interest and value. It is at these times that the client is least guarded and will often unconsciously communicate their thoughts and feelings. As the coach, it is easy for you to be less than fully focused in these moments. As the session begins you might still be thinking about a previous client. At the end your thoughts may stray to the next coaching session or the journey home. You should never relax your attention as a session is just about to begin or when it seems to be over, but should be even more observant than usual.

When does a coaching session really begin and end? It is important to be aware of everything that happens from the moment you meet your client until the moment they are no longer with you.

For example, when arriving for a coaching session a client may make a statement that appears to be merely conversational and nothing to do with the coaching session. They might comment on the weather being 'miserable'. Could they be feeling miserable themselves or did they randomly pick the adjective to describe the rainy day outside? They might say 'I'm feeling hungry'. It might be that they just missed their lunch. However, it could also be that they are unconsciously commenting on their own state of mind, perhaps indicating unconsciously that they are hungry for something other than food – perhaps your attention, perhaps something else. At this point your role is simply to notice these clues, which may or may not be unconscious communications. You can hold in your mind the possibility that they may have some relevance to, or form a connection with, other communications that may emerge as the session unfolds. Maybe they will have relevance and maybe they won't. Your job is to remain open and curious. If and when it becomes appropriate, which might be later in the same session or possibly later in the coaching relationship, you may draw the client's conscious attention to these fragments of unconscious communication.

Door handle moments

Opening remarks can be significant. Similarly, last words often really matter. Time and again a coaching session will be coming towards its end and suddenly, at the last moment, your client will begin to speak about difficult thoughts or feelings, or will reveal something of real importance. This 'door handle moment' is a phenomenon well known to experienced coaches.

Why does this happen so often? Sometimes the client makes a last-minute revelation simply because they know there is no time left to explore it in more detail. This means they can test how it feels to say this out loud, safe in the knowledge that they won't have to go into any further depth right then and there because there isn't time. It can be a way of testing the coach's response to the disclosure and also a way of letting the coach know that this is something the client would like to discuss in a future session.

So, it is important to be especially attentive in the closing moments and the immediate aftermath of a session. Up to this point, you have worked hard to give the client time and to respect their right to progress at their own pace in deciding what to reveal and when to reveal it. You know that they will need to take risks if they are to progress and that this will only happen when they feel safe enough. This will often be at the end of a session. If you can respond warmly to your client bringing important material into the coaching session right at the very end, this will communicate to them that the coaching relationship is a space in which large issues and intense emotions can be safely expressed and explored. You can acknowledge such 'door handle moment' revelations and put them on the agenda to be revisited in the next session, should the client wish. If you respond well to these moments, it can build trust and rapport which will carry forward to the next coaching session and into the whole coaching relationship.

This is another reason why it is so important to stick to time boundaries, to do what you say you are going to do and to end the session when you have said it will end. Knowing that the session will end soon is exactly what creates the special space where the client feels safe to say what they have been wanting to say. Reminders throughout the session as to how much time remains may make it more likely that the last moments of a session will be valuable to your client.

Failing to attend to time boundaries

There can be many reasons for failing to maintain time boundaries. One possibility is that you do not truly value yourself or what you are doing for your clients. It is a challenge for some coaches to realize that they are giving value to their clients simply by being there, creating a thinking space, listening well and asking a limited number of incisive questions. Many coaches also feel that they have not done enough unless they see transformational change in every client in every session. It is worth reminding yourself that often your clients will have been stuck for many years over the issues they bring to coaching. If a coaching intervention results in even a slight movement in a client's thinking, this may be a significant result for them. Another possible cause of loose time boundaries is that you are inclined to take too much responsibility for the outcome. If you feel that you must deliver some benefit before the end of the session, you may end up extending the session to enable you to achieve an outcome.

Some coaches have a tendency to rescue their clients. If you do this, you are not honouring the client's ability to manage themselves and to continue to do the work outside the coaching session. It is easy to overestimate the importance of what you, as the coach, do in the room, as opposed to what the client will do outside the room, in their own time and space. There is a risk of becoming enmeshed with the client and actually impeding their development. Lack of assertiveness or people-pleasing tendencies can be another underlying reason for finding it difficult to manage time effectively. Do you struggle to challenge your client if they regularly arrive late, to end the session on time if your client is in full flow or to say no if your client asks to extend the session? If so, consider whether this is caused by people-pleasing tendencies. You might wish to do some reflective work, using the reflection exercise at the end of this chapter.

When it comes to managing time in coaching sessions, I believe that as coaches we can take some valuable lessons from the therapy profession. The usual approach of the therapist is that the client has bought the therapeutic hour, which in practice is 50 minutes. Sessions always start and finish when scheduled, irrespective of the client. The therapist will dedicate that 'hour' to their client, whether the client is there for the full 50 minutes or not. If the client chooses to arrive ten minutes before the session was scheduled to end, then the client will pay for that whole hour but will have just ten minutes with the therapist. It is also worth noting that for many decades therapists have been working with the most challenging issues and extremes of emotion and believe that this work can and should be done within the fixed time boundary of the therapeutic hour.

There will always be exceptions to any rule. There may be cases where, for very good and specific reasons, agreed time boundaries may be reset or renegotiated in different ways. There are two essentials for any such exceptions. First, they must be clearly contracted with the client, preferably in advance, though sometimes in the moment. Secondly, the coach should have reflected rigorously and honestly and be sure in their own mind that any changes to contracted time boundaries are made to further the goal of coaching, rather than being driven by some of the other factors described in this chapter.

Coaching Exercises

How is your boundary management?

Having been a coaching supervisor for many years, I observe that most issues brought to supervision by coaches stem from the coach having porous boundaries in the coaching relationship. If coaches do not establish clear boundaries at the contracting stage, they can experience resentment when their client shows up late, makes frequent contact outside the sessions, doesn't pay on time or expects to go to the pub with their coach at the end of the session.

How is your own boundary management? It's time to dig deep and be honest with yourself about which boundaries you find it easiest to manage and which of your boundaries are more porous. Consider how you manage boundaries about time, money, support outside of the coaching sessions, levels of intimacy with your client, physical contact and confidentiality.

- Which boundaries of your own do you find hardest to respect when you are coaching?
- Which of your client's boundaries do you find hardest to respect?
- What actions can you take to improve your boundary management?

Busy fool or focused and effective?

For one week each month, keep a detailed diary of all your work commitments and activities. At the end of the week have a careful look at how you spent your time. How do you feel about it? What surprises you? Have you been busy or effective? How have your actions this week taken you towards your business goals? What have you done which has given the biggest return on investment? What has taken the biggest chunk of your time? What have you done, which you didn't need to do? Work out how much income you have generated during this week and then calculate what your hourly rate has been for the week. What changes can you make to improve how you manage and value your time?

Suggested Further Reading

Casement, P. (1985) *On Learning from the Patient*. London and New York: Tavistock Publications.
Cloud, H. and Townsend, J. (2007) *Boundaries*. Grand Rapids, MI: Zondervan.
Passmore, J. (2011) *Supervision in Coaching: Supervision, Ethics and Continuous Professional Development*. London: Kogan Page Limited.

7 Facilitating Change

Supporting or facilitating behaviour change can be a complex process, which may require the coach to work with the client to identify a desired change or a goal, and to evaluate their readiness for change and explore what they are currently doing either to support the desired change or to inhibit it. This chapter explores the subject of transformational change, identifying some of the conditions that facilitate it and how these core elements can be integrated into the coaching process. It explores ways of uncovering the hidden commitments and assumptions that stand in the way of change, how to recognize when a client's limiting beliefs are preventing them from changing and what you can do to challenge such beliefs in your clients.

The Difference Between Change and Transformation

Changing the habits and behaviours of a lifetime is a challenge. Your role is to help clients build their resourcefulness to make change happen. If change happened easily, your clients would have already done it by themselves and would not be coming to you for help. Every client is different in their readiness for change and in their motivation. Some clients lack the knowledge, support or skill to make a change. Sometimes if a client changes, it will have a significant impact on their wider system, their family members, their colleagues or their way of life. In many cases, there will be costs to making a change as well as benefits. Clients may be unaware that the unacknowledged benefits of their current situation are keeping them from changing.

Other coaching clients have deep-seated limiting beliefs or a lifetime's worth of conditioning which keep them doing what they have always done. Some clients can pinpoint the precise moment when they developed a belief which is still holding them back and perhaps even blighting their lives. Others are unaware of all the factors preventing them from making the changes they say they want. Some clients may be under pressure from others to change, and this may mean that they lack the intrinsic motivation. They may have to face some tough decisions – change and compromise their values to stay in their relationship or job role or elect not to change and risk losing their job or relationship.

I meet coaches all the time who are criticizing themselves for not achieving enough life-changing, transformational moments for their clients. Here are some of the questions they ask me:

- Should the goal of coaching sessions always be transformational change?
- Can you consider the coaching sessions to be a success if your client simply takes some small, practical steps?
- Can change be merely behavioural or does long-lasting change always require a belief shift?
- Is it within the realms of coaching to address a client's limiting beliefs, which may involve exploring their past, or would this only be appropriate during therapy?

To facilitate transformation, you need to understand the psychology of change, what enables change, what holds us back from changing and what part you can play in supporting your client's change process. Understanding and enabling change form the essence of coaching. More important than familiarity with the tools and techniques you use is understanding why you are using them and how they will speed up the process.

The way you approach the change process with your clients is key to achieving a successful outcome. This begins with your own beliefs, assumptions and attitudes. How do you know which tools or techniques, or approaches will work best? How do you know how quickly to work or how far to push your client towards change? How do you balance championing, challenging, checking progress and managing accountability with compassion and understanding for your client? How do you manage your client's response – and your own responses – if your client does not achieve the change they want?

How Change Happens

Case Study 7.1: Betty

Betty has been coaching for just over a year. She specializes in coaching owners of family businesses. Betty favours a non-directive approach to coaching and is not keen on goal-setting. She sees the coaching sessions as a safe space in which her clients can think and talk about anything they want, in the presence of a trusted confidante. 'I just don't think it's my job as coach to pressurize my client to achieve outcomes or to check up on their progress. They are adults, after all', she says. 'I'm not sure that any of my clients make real changes but I think they enjoy being listened to without judgement and they feel recharged to go back into the workplace, which is helpful. On the other hand, I wonder if I could be doing more to help my clients achieve transformation or even make longer-term changes. Should I be aiming for more "light-bulb" moments? I do sometimes feel as though all we are doing is having a cosy chat.'

There is no obligation to set goals, check on progress and push for transformation with your clients. It all depends on how you have contracted to work with them. It is perfectly acceptable for coaches to have a contract with a client that consists of offering a listening ear, a thinking environment and a safe space. If Betty in Case Study 7.1 has contracted clearly with her client, then both parties have agreed to that way of working. Betty also needs to be sure in her own mind that her approach is based on the belief that the environment and the relationship she creates with the client are the right conditions for the client to grow, develop and change.

There are many ways in which change can occur in clients and there is a wide spectrum of coaching approaches that can facilitate change, self-awareness and growth. Indeed, there are very many models and theories about how change happens and, as a trained coach, you probably learned about different change models on your coach training programme and may well have some favourites of your own. In using any model, it is crucial to know why you are using it and how it fits into your chosen approach. Change models can be useful guides but should be used flexibly, with a light steer. All models will have their limitations and there will be exceptions to any model, particularly for models which predict stages of change. People don't always go through the stages in the same order and they can skip stages too. Being too wedded to a model can limit the flexibility of your coaching and prevent you from honouring the uniqueness of your client's individual experience of change.

The Common Elements In Facilitating Change

Most change models cover similar elements, although they may be expressed in different terms and they may appear in different sequences in each of the models. Some models represent stages of the change process and others a process for facilitating change. When I am coaching clients through change, I find it useful to think about addressing all these different elements, instead of following a sequential process:

- Readiness to change
- The gap between the current reality and the desired change
- Experimentation, practice and action
- The role of the coach in facilitating change

Readiness to change

Clients come to us in all different states of readiness to change. Some clients have been 'told' to change by a third party, others think they want to change but are not sure if they want it enough. Some clients know they want to change but don't know how to do it and others are looking for a change but don't know exactly what it should be.

All these clients would require different approaches from a coach and different coaching questions, such as:

- What would move you from thinking that you should do this to thinking that you would love to do this?
- What will it cost you to do this? What will it cost you if you don't do it?
- What will you gain if you do this? What will you gain if you don't do this?
- What is one compelling reason to stay where you are and one compelling reason to make the change?
- What do you need to change in your life to be ready for this change?

The gap between the current reality and the desired change

If a client is saying that they want to change but they have not made it happen, it is essential to explore which obstacles are in their way. These may be internal obstacles, such as beliefs and assumptions, confidence levels or values, or they may be external factors, such as time, money, skill level, other people. A useful approach to exploring obstacles is the Obstacle Analysis Grid (Neill 2006).

This model identifies the nine major life obstacles which prevent us from making the changes we want. The categories are: information, skills, belief, well-being, motivation, other people, time, money and fear. You can score yourself from 1 to 10 (10 being an area of strength) in each of the categories to determine which are the areas in which you feel less strong and are therefore blockers to your desired change, or you can write a statement in each category. In Case Study 7.2, my client scored and commented on each of the categories.

Case Study 7.2: Amy

I used the following grid when I coached Amy. Amy was having coaching because she had turned down opportunities for promotion in her company. Her manager had identified her as a talented employee and had put her on a talent programme. She was great at her job but was not fulfilling her potential, and her line manager was baffled. She completed the Obstacle Analysis Grid with me in the first session:

Information	Skill	Belief
9 – I think I am aware of what a promotion would mean.	9 – I have most of the technical skills to take the next step.	5 – Not sure I have the right personality to be a leader.

Well-being	Other people	Motivation
5 – I am worried that I won't be able to cope with the stress.	4 – There are members of my team who I would have to manage if I got the promotion. I am not sure I am strong enough to manage them.	9 – I want to progress in my career.
Time	**Money**	**Fear**
9 – Time is no problem.	9 – More money appeals to me but I am financially secure already.	5 – I am frightened I will be unpopular with my team members.

Completing this exercise gave both me and Amy a lot of useful information at a glance. We spent several sessions exploring all the reasons for Amy's doubt about her leadership ability and fear of being disliked by team members, and the worry that her well-being would suffer. Looking at this grid, it was no surprise that Amy was resisting going for promotion. She had not been able to express any of this explicitly to her manager, but she said that the headings and the ratings helped her.

We focused on the link between the comments in the categories: Belief, Fear, Other people and Well-being. I wondered how Amy's assumptions about leadership, unpopularity and stress had come about. Amy soon told me that she and her best friend had been in the running for the Head Girl position at school and Amy had got it. Her best friend reacted by bullying Amy and turning all her friends against her. Amy had experienced a stress reaction, taken time off school and had given up being Head Girl. The school then gave it to her best friend. Looking at the grid, the similarities seemed obvious between Amy's childhood experience and her current situation, but Amy hadn't made the link before. We worked together for several months to build Amy's confidence and to challenge the way in which she had developed a generalized, universal belief from a single, specific childhood incident. Amy developed a more balanced view about becoming a leader. She had her eyes open to the potential pitfalls of taking a promotion. She recognized that some people might be difficult or envious of her, but she believed she now had sufficient personal resources to deal with any challenges.

Desire and commitment to changing

When someone has declared themselves ready to change, it doesn't always mean that they are prepared for the energy and effort it can take. Whenever I have had therapy, I have noticed how therapists mention that changing can be hard work.

I sometimes wonder whether, as coaches, we have a tendency to underplay the commitment it takes.

The Transtheoretical Model of Change, developed by Prochaska and DiClemente (1982), is used widely by professionals working in the areas of health and addiction, where their clients are struggling to change. Stage 3 of the model is about preparing emotionally for the change. This preparation entails building resilience, building in contingency for disappointment or relapse, and acknowledging what price you might pay for making the change.

Questions to ask are:

- How important is this to you?
- What are you prepared to sacrifice to achieve the change?
- What support do you need to do this, and from whom?
- What will be the benefit to you of achieving this change?
- What could cause you to give up and how would you overcome a setback?
- How will you reward yourself for the progress you are making?

Experimentation, practice and action

> The first problem for all of us, men and women, is not to learn, but to unlearn.
> (Gloria Steinem 1970)

We begin all our coach training programmes with reference to Gloria Steinem's quote. It acknowledges that course delegates will have to get out of their old familiar patterns and habits of communicating, as well as learning new skills. Old habits may even include interrupting and giving unsolicited advice, and new skills will include: listening, questioning and being able to tolerate a state of 'not knowing' with their clients. Bringing about change requires learning new skills and behaviours and unlearning old ones.

Even when clients are ready, willing and able to make the change, it can still take time and repeated practice to adopt new behaviours. I think 'habit' should be included in Michael Neill's Obstacle Analysis Grid (2006). It is easy to underestimate our neurological and physical hardwiring and need for familiarity.

I once worked with a client who realized that he was, in his words, 'a doormat and a pushover'. He had been bullied, abused and manipulated and he wanted, and needed, to become more assertive. We did all the necessary groundwork – building on his strengths and developing his self-esteem. He had taken a long hard look at what could be the consequences of not changing. He knew why he wanted to change and how much he wanted it. Yet he still said 'yes' when he meant to say 'no'. He still needed to be liked at any cost. He bowed and scraped and apologized to everyone.

I was frustrated and stuck. Then I had a 'eureka' moment when I was at home in my kitchen. I had recently moved my kitchen bin. I had decided to move it; I wanted to move it. I could see that it had moved, and yet every time I went to throw something away, I walked to where the bin used to be. I did this for many days. I thought about my client. I recognized that he had 50 years of hardwiring and habitual patterns of behaviour holding him back from changing something far more important than relocating a bin. I realized that he had to practise some new habits repeatedly and gradually. I began by inviting my client to say 'no' to me, in the safety of the coaching session. He found it very difficult but the more he did it, the easier it became. I invited him to give me some negative feedback about my coaching, to tell me what aspects of the session he hadn't enjoyed. He squirmed and tried to wriggle out of it, but I held firm until he eventually told me what he really thought. Over time, I challenged him to say 'no' more often to friends and family. He proudly arrived one day telling me that he had refused three things that week: to attend a social function at work, to sign up for a loyalty card in a store and to babysit his sister's children so she could go out drinking. He grew in confidence over months as the new behaviours started to feel familiar.

The role of the coach in facilitating change

Studies of transformational learning have identified factors which are consistently present when change happens, or the factors which are missing when it does not happen. Jack Mezirow (1991: 193) suggests that the following situations give rise to critical self-reflection which can lead to transformational learning:

- A disorienting dilemma
- A state of puzzlement
- The recognition that others share our feelings
- The presence of an empathetic provocateur (an interesting alternative word for a coach)

In 1995, Peter Jarvis coined the term 'non-learning' for our response to everyday experience. He proposed the idea that when our experience conforms to our mental models or our expectations, then no learning or change happens.

My understanding of these findings, put simply, is that if things tick along in the usual way, our thinking is not challenged. When we are faced with difficult and new situations, or if we are challenged by someone who has our best interests at heart, we can be jolted into reviewing some of our thoughts and behaviours. When we realize that we are not alone in feeling the way we do, our situation can become normalized to the extent that we no longer think it is irresolvable or that we are uniquely flawed in some way. This recognition that others share our feelings can lead us to seek out ways to change.

Case Study 7.3: George

George came to Chloe for coaching to help him achieve more balance in his life. George was a successful entrepreneur, who admitted to being 'a workaholic'. Chloe noticed that he used this term with a sense of pride. George's goals were to work two days per week, cut down his drinking, play more golf and book an extended holiday with his wife. Although George insisted 'Life's too short to work all the time. None of us know how long we have on this earth so we have to enjoy it while we are here', Chloe didn't see any evidence of real desire to change. She felt that George's motivation was extrinsic: it was the right thing to say because other people wanted him to slow down.

Chloe worked hard to develop George's intrinsic motivation to change. When their coaching programme came to an end, George had made some small changes to his work–life balance. He played golf a bit more and left the office at lunchtime on Fridays. George persuaded Chloe that these small steps were a promising start to him achieving his goal, although Chloe's gut feeling said otherwise. A year later, George returned to see Chloe. He was recovering from major heart surgery, following a cardiac arrest. George now realized what his lifestyle had cost him and told Chloe, 'Now I'm ready to do the work to make sure I never go back to the way I used to live my life'. Chloe berated herself for not having worked harder to increase George's readiness and motivation to change. She wondered what more she could have done and whether she should have pushed harder to show George what the consequences of his lifestyle could be. She acknowledged that she had let George's strong personality overpower her. Chloe asked George for permission to challenge him more in her coaching this time around.

Coaching can reproduce the elements which give rise to transformational learning, as identified by Mezirow (1991). The coach, providing both empathy and provocation, invites the client to think new thoughts and to review their long-held assumptions about themselves and the world at large. Maybe in the coaching sessions, the client learns that they are not alone in feeling how they do and that others share their feelings. Coaching clients are no longer in a state of 'non-learning', as Jarvis (1995: 27:1, 24–35) calls it. Now they have a coach who is challenging, championing, encouraging, provoking and holding them to account to reconsider and re-evaluate their lives.

Erik de Haan (2008) identified that critical moments occur in the coaching relationship when tensions, uncertainties and anxieties arise, when a particular vulnerability is examined, when the coaching relationship is put to the test or when the coach accesses their own emotions. Coaching someone to change is a valiant endeavour. Your role is to validate your client's feelings and balance an acceptance of their current situation with a belief that change is possible. This increases the chance of evoking their resourcefulness. Simultaneously you will want to hold them accountable, while acknowledging that relapse is perfectly possible. When you do this, the conversation is far from a cosy chat. A coaching relationship that supports a client to change their behaviours, however small the changes may be, needs to be dynamic, supportive and different from the client's daily experiences, and it needs to be informed, on the coach's side, by a theoretical understanding of how change happens. The coach needs to ask the client what will be the benefits of changing and what will be the costs, for themselves and for the wider systems in which they exist. The change work needs to encompass the three overlapping domains of thoughts, feelings and behaviours and to examine beliefs or assumptions which are either supporting or inhibiting the change.

Transformational learning involves changes in the feelings, values and attitudes which shape our thinking and behaviour. A coach has to understand what motivates the client. For example, are they motivated more by threat (away from what they don't want) or by reward (towards what they do want)? Are they motivated in the same way in all contexts? For example, someone may be motivated by the promise of success when building their business but be motivated away from being over-weight and unhealthy when taking up exercise. Understanding the subtle distinctions of an individual's motivational traits can make a big difference to how the coach is able to motivate their client. In most change models, there is the mention of a trigger for change, and that is sometimes a puzzling or disorienting event, as for George in Case Study 7.3. Sometimes the trigger is the presence of a facilitator of some kind – a coach or an empathetic provocateur. Sometimes the coach creates the trigger by asking a specifically challenging coaching question or giving direct feedback to the client to jolt them out of an assumption they hold. Change is unlikely to occur unless something new or different is happening in the coaching session, which doesn't happen in the rest of the client's life. The coach needs to be fully engaged in the process at an emotional level and this sometimes means declaring their feelings to the client and being prepared to provoke or challenge in the coaching session. For some clients the change doesn't happen in the coaching room, but outside, when the client has had time to process the experience of the coaching session.

Working with Limiting Beliefs

Case Study 7.4: Jo

Jo has been coaching for 18 months. She had a long and successful career in banking before starting her own coaching business. She coaches managers and senior managers in the financial services sector. Jo has had positive feedback about her coaching from her clients and their organizations, but she feels increasingly that she is working at surface level. Jo says:

> I often pick up clues that my coaching clients have some limiting beliefs that are getting in the way of them changing or progressing in their careers. But if I'm honest, I shy away from addressing underlying issues of this kind. I work with commercially

minded, hard-nosed people who mostly don't feel comfortable talking about their feelings, let alone exploring childhood stuff. I am wondering whether I should be looking at my clients' limiting beliefs, but I'm not entirely sure how to do it – particularly in a corporate context. I'm worried that it feels a bit close to therapy and I might open a can of worms or do some damage. Are there any tried and tested coaching techniques for changing limiting beliefs which would be suitable to use in a business context? Also, how do I introduce the subject to people who are not very open to self-discovery?

Coaching has undergone rapid growth and change since its emergence in the 1990s. One significant change that has occurred is the move towards approaches underpinned by psychology and a consequent blurring of the lines between coaching and counselling or therapy. When coaching first emerged, it grew out of four different movements: the 'talking' therapies, consulting and organizational development, the personal development movement and sports coaching. In its early days coaching sought to differentiate itself from its origins and to define itself by what it was not, rather than by what it was. Coaches proudly stated that coaching was 'none of the above', but something else that had taken the best bits from all the other disciplines and created a new and powerful 'helping by talking' methodology. The coaching industry was particularly keen to distance itself from any association with in-depth psychological work or therapeutic approaches. However, as coaching has matured and developed, so has the realization that the personal and professional are inextricably linked and that it is not useful for either the coach or the client to try to separate them.

Coaches working in businesses regularly find themselves dealing with issues that are negatively affecting their clients' lives, such as redundancy, divorce, bereavement, low self-esteem, lack of assertiveness, stress and anxiety, as well as limiting beliefs.

Early coach training was not rooted in theory and relied heavily on basic goal-setting frameworks. Since then, the realization that coaches cannot avoid working with the whole person has meant that professional coaching bodies and educators of coaches are seeking greater psychological underpinning for coaching interventions and the inclusion of psychological concepts in coach training. Coaching continues to be an unregulated sector and, although there is movement towards professionalization, progress is slow. However, it is now apparent that coaches cannot avoid working on blocks in the client's thinking, feeling, behaviours or beliefs if they wish to enable the client to achieve mobility and development. Most of these blocks include some limiting beliefs or assumptions.

It is now widely accepted that coaches need to be able to work with the whole person, and this includes working with any limiting beliefs and assumptions that are holding their clients back from achieving what they want. Some coaches, like Jo in Case Study 7.4, are still concerned about whether this is straying into the domain of therapy. My view, on the contrary, is that dealing with limiting beliefs sits at the core of most coaching work. How many of us do not harbour some limiting assumptions which would benefit from being re-examined and questioned in a safe and mutually respectful relationship? How can we make lasting behavioural change without changing the beliefs, assumptions and attitudes which drive our thoughts and behaviours?

Your initial contracting conversations are key. All coaches should have clear conversations about what they are offering and how the boundaries will be managed throughout the coaching relationship. This will include an honest discussion about the inevitably blurred lines between coaching and therapy. You also need to have an ability to notice possible indications of a psychological or mental health issue and have the confidence to discuss this with the client so that you can agree on the best course of action. You will need clear guidelines about when to refer a client on to other professionals if you ever feel that the work is outside the limits of your expertise. This also means being familiar with and understanding the ethical standards and requirements of the coaching body to which you belong.

What are limiting beliefs and how do we work with them?

Limiting beliefs or assumptions hold us back from achieving what we want, and they often limit our self-esteem too. Limiting beliefs are generally formed in childhood and are usually beliefs about ourselves (e.g. 'I'm not a leader, more of a follower'); other people (e.g. 'Most people can't be trusted'); or the world at large (e.g. 'The world is a dangerous place'). Holding these beliefs prevents us from doing things we would do if we had more positive beliefs. When we are young, we are told that adults, parents, teachers and older siblings know more than we do and that we should listen to what they say. Children have no reference points of their own, so they tend to believe whatever adults tell them. Coupled with this, children's minds are open and receptive to almost any suggestion given to them. So, if children receive the messages that they are not good enough, naughty, unlovable, clumsy, no good at maths or slow at reading, from people whose opinions they trust, these can become unquestionable truths, sometimes lasting long into adulthood, especially if they also elicit a powerful emotional response – fear, shame or guilt.

Limiting beliefs are formed in a number of ways. Sometimes there is one defining moment, perhaps being told off in front of your classmates, or failing an important exam. Some children experience labelling, being known as 'the naughty one' or 'the hard-working one'. Often the intention behind these messages is good, for instance, telling a child not to boast, but children do not have the ability to discern this at the time. Children also learn more from what their parents do than from what their parents tell them to do. If your parents believe the world is an unsafe place, you are likely to believe that too. Often children misunderstand the meaning of what is said to them. For example, I had a client who had low self-esteem and believed herself to be physically unattractive. When she was young, her friends called her 'Pat the dog' and she had understood this to mean that she was not good-looking. Until she was encouraged to re-examine this from an adult perspective, she had never realized that it was, in fact, just a play on words and nothing to do with her physical appearance.

Recognizing limiting beliefs

How do you recognize when a client has a belief which is limiting them? Watch out for repeated statements about themselves, about others or about the world around them that are expressed as unquestionable, fixed truths. Listen out particularly for words like 'always' and 'everyone'. Notice any discrepancy between your view of your client and their own self-concept. Some clients remember well the defining moments which triggered their limiting beliefs and are aware of these beliefs but do not know how to change them.

Most coaching conversations about limiting beliefs and assumptions can be approached with a light steer once a strong relationship of trust is in place between coach and client. It can be useful to share with your client information about how beliefs are formed, as this can normalize their own situation for them.

How to work with limiting beliefs

The first stage is to identify the belief. Ask your client what they believe or assume about the topic which is stopping them from moving forward. Let them come up with as many beliefs or assumptions as they want. When did they first develop this belief? Did the belief come from someone else? A key factor in belief change is to encourage your client to question and review the belief with adult experience, wisdom and logic. Perhaps for the first time the client will be able to question whether the belief was true once, and whether it is still true today.

Help your client identify what they habitually think, say and do which perpetuates the belief. Encourage them to think about the person who was instrumental in setting up this belief for them and ask them to consider, as an adult, whether this person is someone they now trust and respect. Invite your client to seek to understand what the person's intention was, at that time.

You can also ask your client to look back with compassion on the child they were, to consider what resources they had available to them when they were young and to remind themselves what resources they have now, as an adult, that can help them. Ask your client what they would like to say to their younger self, as the adult they are today. Ask them what payoff they get from holding on to the limiting belief and what it costs them to have this belief.

I've worked with several clients who have limiting beliefs about their capability and who lack confidence in themselves. In our coaching sessions, they have acknowledged that the benefit or payoff to holding these beliefs is that they manage other people's expectations of them by telling others that they are not very good at something. This often results in them receiving lots of praise, attention and affirmation from others. It can also keep them safe from criticism as they criticize themselves before anyone else can. The costs can be: not developing to reach their full potential, avoiding challenges and growth opportunities and, eventually, convincing others of their lack of ability.

Ask your client what they would do differently if they had some more empowering beliefs.

Invite them to gather the opinions of people they really trust and respect about their limiting belief and to reflect on the ways other people perceive them.

Working with belief change requires dogged determination. You will need to keep chipping away at the belief over time. Do not expect it to disappear overnight. Use gentle humour and lightness and even be a little provocative. You can try agreeing with the client's belief and see how they respond – it may prompt them to reject it. Your role as coach is to be honest and congruent in everything you do with your client, so they trust that you mean it when you praise, support and champion them and also when you challenge them. If clients think you just say nice things to them because you are a coach, they will not believe you when you challenge their limiting beliefs.

Coaching Exercises for Working with Limiting Beliefs

Free association list

This powerful exercise enables you to explore your beliefs about any given topic. It is non-threatening and suitable for a corporate coaching context. As a coach, it is an exercise that you can complete for any number of topics where you are encountering resistance or difficulty.

Take a sheet of paper and write at the top the topic about which you have some limiting beliefs or assumptions. Topics can be general or specific, for example:

- Public speaking
- Networking
- My relationship with my boss
- Me as a leader
- Anything else about which you have limiting beliefs

Sit quietly on your own and write a list of words, thoughts and phrases which come into your head when you think about this topic. Let the words flow and don't over-think them. This is a free association exercise in which you allow words and thoughts to come. Don't edit, either in your mind or on paper – put down everything that comes into your head, even if it seems bizarre. Stop writing when you find that you are thinking too hard about the next thing to write.

Now look at the list and ask yourself the following questions:

- What does this list say to me about my beliefs about [the topic]?
- Which words on the list are useful to me?
- Which words on the list are limiting me?

Now look at the limiting words, thoughts or phrases and ask the following questions:

- Whose words are they? Have they been said to me before in my life? By whom?
- Are they true? Do I actually believe them?
- Which words, thoughts or phrases would be more helpful to me?

Finally, replace the limiting words or phrases with new phrases which are helpful and empowering to you and which sit comfortably with you as realistic replacements.

Review the amended list and, as you read it to yourself, check for any signs of discomfort. If any of the words make you feel uncomfortable, amend them again so that you eventually feel at ease with all the words on the list.

Try on the finished list for size, reading it to yourself one last time. What could you do differently with the new set of beliefs, words and thoughts about your chosen topic? What different behaviours would be possible for you?

'Post-it' note exercise

This exercise allows you and your client to deal with potentially emotional or difficult beliefs with a light touch. The use of Post-it notes, which are such a familiar and everyday piece of stationery, adds to the sense of safety. The movement and creativity it involves can be energizing and cathartic. I have seen clients with Post-it notes stuck all over themselves and covering the walls of a room.

The exercise is also memorable because it engages emotion and all the senses. Clients can take the Post-it notes with them as a visual reminder too.

Ask your client to write down, on Post-it notes, beliefs about themselves and labels they wear or have worn, whether empowering or limiting. Labels usually take the form of qualities or failings that have been attributed to them as a child by other people. For example, they may have been 'the sensible one', 'the sporty one', 'a slow learner'. When your client has written until they can't think of any more beliefs or labels, ask them to examine each one in turn and question it. Is it true? Do I think it is true? Was it true once? Is it still true? Is it helpful to me? Where did it come from and how reliable was the 'witness'? This last question is important because part of the process of wearing away a limiting belief is to challenge the intention or the authority of the person who first delivered that message.

As your client goes through the beliefs in turn, invite them to do one of four things with each Post-it:

- Keep it if it serves them well.
- Rewrite it in their own words so that it is more appealing or useful to them but retains the essence of the meaning. This is particularly useful if they feel there is some truth in the message but they find the words unkind. For example, someone who was given the label 'shy' may prefer to rewrite it as 'discerning'.

- Destroy it. I have seen Post-it notes torn into pieces, scrunched up and thrown in the rubbish bin, stamped on and even set on fire (not to be advised). This can be a highly energetic and empowering stage of the process.
- Replace it by writing some new positive beliefs, which they had not thought of before. This stage can be an opportunity for you to join in with some suggestions of qualities which you have noticed in them.

Like the Post-it notes themselves, the learning from this exercise tends to stick. However, also like the Post-it notes, it can be unstuck. Remember that working with belief change usually requires some repeated and gentle chipping away at the limiting belief, and this exercise is part of that process. There is also a chance that you may get lucky and find that the Post-it note exercise is all you need.

Suggested Further Reading

Dilts, R. (1990) *Changing Belief Systems with Neuro-Linguistic Programming.* Scotts Valley, CA: Dilts Strategy Group.

Kelly, R. and Allen, C. (2011) *Thrive.* Cambridge: Rob Kelly Publishing.

Leary-Joyce, J. (2014) *The Fertile Void: Gestalt Coaching at Work.* London: AoEC Press.

Prochaska, J.O. and Prochaska, J.M. (2016) *Changing to Thrive: Overcome the Top Risks to Lasting Health and Happiness.* Center City, MN: Hazelden Publishing.

8 Group Coaching

Sometimes, coaches with no experience of facilitation or training find themselves being asked to coach a group or a team. I have known coaches to say 'yes' to this and then quickly try to acquire the knowledge and skills required to coach more than one person, particularly if the focus of their coach training was on one-to-one coaching. This chapter looks at the benefits of group coaching, the different forms it can take, and the similarities and differences with one-to-one coaching. The chapter also explores what skills and experience you need to coach a group of people, the difference between a team and a group, how to maintain a coaching attitude versus a trainer's attitude when coaching a group of people and what additional support you might need when coaching more than one person.

Coaching More than One Person

Many coach training courses focus on one-to-one coaching, and yet surveys and reports on the coaching industry suggest that only a small percentage of coaches earn their income exclusively from one-to-one coaching. The 2016 ICF Global Coaching Survey (2016: 23) found that 94 per cent of external, freelance coaches offer additional services besides coaching, for instance, training, consultancy and facilitation.

I have run coaching groups for people who lacked confidence, for parents and for women returning to work after maternity leave. I've also run coaching groups for delegates on a graduate programme in an organization, for owners of small businesses and for first-time line managers at work. I have run coaching groups at an adult education centre, which attracted a range of people who all wanted something different from the programme but shared an interest in experiencing some coaching for themselves. Sometimes, what starts out as a one-to-one coaching assignment can change. For example, a client who is having one-to-one coaching about a difficult work relationship may eventually ask their coach to provide a joint coaching session with a colleague to enable them to discuss their difficulties in a controlled environment, facilitated by the coach.

All these scenarios involving coaching more than one person require careful consideration, an ability to recognize the extent of your coaching experience and your competence in this area. Alongside this, you will need to fully understand the client's goals and be able to make an assessment about the most appropriate intervention for the client. It may be that mediation, team building, conflict resolution or training interventions are more appropriate than team or group coaching.

What is a group?

A group is often described as a collection of individuals who share a common interest, which joins them together in some way. Group members have individual goals, individual areas of focus and are individually accountable for the achievement of those goals. They are independent of one another, although they may still sometimes work together to complete a group task. They can develop a common, group identity. Group members share information with one another and provide support for fellow group members.

What is a team?

A team is a collection of individuals who have come together, or been brought together, to fulfil a core goal or purpose. Achievement of the common goal requires the joint commitment and contribution of all team members. Team members are interdependent. Team members share responsibility for the team task and are jointly accountable for the achievement of the task. The success or failure of common goals is shared and felt by members of the team. At its best, a team is capable of achieving results beyond those which could be achieved by the group of individuals.

Coaching Groups – What Additional Skills do you Need?

In the same way as one-to-one coaching is underpinned by an understanding of human psychology and motivation, you will need an understanding of group dynamics if you are planning to coach more than one person at a time. If you have been trained as a facilitator of groups, you will almost certainly be aware of some models and theories about group dynamics. You will probably have learned skills for managing difficulty or conflict within a group too. For coaches with no experience of managing groups, I recommend further training and skills development in group work and facilitation.

As a field of study, group dynamics has its roots in psychology and sociology. Studies of groups have included social groups, family groups and work groups, and several studies have looked at groups in extreme situations, such as warfare, to understand how groups operate in challenging situations. In group dynamics, there is a general acceptance that the whole is greater than the sum of its parts. Group dynamics theories explore mechanisms for dealing with status, leadership, ostracism of group members, inclusion of members and group decision-making processes.

If you are offering group coaching in an organizational setting, you will also need a grasp of organizational life and the competing demands on individuals of working within a complex system. You will need an ability to work without bias or judgement and deliver feedback with integrity, and to use clear, adult communication. You should be able to think on your feet, work under pressure and have the confidence to deal with challenging situations in the group. You will need tact and resilience to enable you to forge good relationships with different members of the group. It is important for you to have sufficient presence and credibility to hold the respect of the group members. You need to be able to establish clear boundaries and to provide a safe space for everyone in the group, while being guided by the professional ethics of your work.

A basic understanding of adult learning principles is a prerequisite for group coaches. Adults bring a range of personal, professional and life experiences with them when they enter a learning environment. They filter new information through the knowledge and experiences they already have, and they form opinions of their own. When you are running group coaching sessions, ensure that you use the experience and expertise within the group.

Adults are self-motivated and self-directed to learn, and they benefit from having an input into the coaching process, ground rules and ways of working. Agree on ways of working together and give group members permission to co-create the agenda or the focus of the sessions.

Adults need their coaching and learning experiences to be grounded in reality, working on real-life work and personal issues. The group coaching experience needs to be relevant to the group members' lives and work.

Coaching Teams – Even More Skills Required

Case Study 8.1: Teresa

Teresa has been coaching for three years and has developed a niche offering, providing one-to-one coaching in professional services firms. She has worked with one small firm for just over a year and has coached all four partners individually. There is some conflict in the partnership and Teresa has now been asked if she would be prepared to coach all the partners together as a team to help them resolve the conflict. Teresa can see that this could be beneficial, but she has no previous experience of working with teams, and her coach training focused just on one-to-one work. Teresa is wondering whether she needs specific qualifications in facilitation, mediation or team coaching before she can think about coaching all the partners together. She is also worried about how to remain impartial as she already knows the partners individually and has better relationships with some than others. Teresa is worried about the expectation that she would be able to help the partners resolve their conflict, as this is not an area of expertise for her.

I have supervised several coaches who have found themselves agreeing to coach two or three business partners together, to coach a team or even to coach a married couple. 'How difficult can it be?', one of these coaches naïvely thought to himself before embarking on a team coaching assignment. It didn't take long for him to realize that the psychological and personal inter-dynamics of coaching teams are even more complex than those of groups. In team coaching you are focusing simultaneously on the individuals, the relationships between them and the development and performance of the team, or system, as a whole. There will be a need to manage group dynamics in group coaching, but you are not having to focus on the performance and development of the group as a system outside of the coaching sessions. Team coaching requires a whole range of additional skills, knowledge and confidence. If, like Teresa in Case Study 8.1, you are contemplating coaching a team of people, you will also need to be prepared to encounter open conflict or conflict simmering away beneath the surface. I remember once being asked by an organization, not to provide a team coaching session but to provide 'a controlled explosion'. You will also need to develop a deep understanding of your own history of experiences in teams and your relationship with conflict. If you have not had previous experience of working with teams, it will be essential to get further training before offering team coaching sessions.

Group Coaching

Case Study 8.2: Tom

Tom has been finding it difficult to get enough one-to-one coaching clients to provide him with the income he needs. He has had the idea of running some coaching groups. He plans to get six people together in a coaching group – people from a variety of backgrounds, businesses or sectors, all of whom are looking for some coaching to achieve personal or professional goals. He plans to coach them as a group, teach them some coaching models and techniques and encourage them to coach one another and create a supportive network in which they can each grow and develop as individuals. Tom thinks that this will be a cost-effective solution for people who want one-to-one coaching but who find the fees prohibitive. He has experience of training and facilitating but has not run coaching groups before. Tom still has lots of questions: What are the benefits of group coaching? How can he ensure that everyone in the group benefits equally from the experience? How can he maintain a coaching role with more than one person? What is the ideal size of a coaching group? Does he need a structure for each session or should he respond to the needs of the group? Would it be better to work on his own or with another coach?

Group coaching is on the rise and not only for reasons of affordability. Coaching groups work because a small group of individuals with a shared interest, or with the same needs, can come together to share experiences and learn about their own and others' dilemmas, aspirations and goals. Members of coaching groups can offer one another support, encouragement and accountability to meet their individual goals. Coaching groups often serve to normalize an individual's situation because members find that they are not alone and that others in the group have similar concerns or experiences. There can also be a valuable amount of knowledge-sharing within a coaching group and they offer great networking opportunities too. Coaching groups learn together. The individual members often acquire a coaching style, by a kind of osmosis, even if it has not been explicitly taught to them. Members of coaching groups can find that they transfer their new-found coaching skills to other areas of their lives, almost without knowing they are doing it. From a business perspective, it is an effective way to grow your coaching practice more quickly. You will be helping more people at any one time and growing your client base more quickly, which will provide you with more opportunities for testimonials and referrals to new clients. You may also find that group coaching enables you to work fewer hours for the same income. If you are thinking about starting a coaching group, you will need to determine what will be the focus of your coaching group and what needs or circumstances the group members will share. An ideal number for a coaching group is between six and eight people.

It will also be useful to create a structure or framework for your group coaching sessions. There should be enough flexibility in the framework for you to be able to respond to the group's specific needs and offer a bespoke experience when required.

An example structure for a group coaching session would be:

- Welcome/introductions
- Ground rules and ways of working
- Check in/update by group members
- Input of a coaching model and coaching in pairs or threes
- Shared learning and commitments from the session
- Check out by group members

The joy of group coaching

Many years ago, when I finished a psychotherapy training programme, the tutors marked the ending of the course by telling each of the students in turn what gift they would like to give them. When it was my turn, they said, 'We wish you many groups for the rest of your life.' At the time, I was perplexed. I had just spent several years learning how to work one-to-one with clients. However, over the following years, I learned that they were right. I feel energized by working with groups; I love the interactions within the group and my interactions with the whole group. I delight in the way the group supports and champions individual members to be the best they can be. I love how the group develops its own identity and I enjoy the in-jokes and the shared language which the group acquires. I enjoy how the groups, month by month, begin to self-manage and become less reliant on my input. You will know if you are someone who finds joy in working with groups. Maybe you notice that you feel more exhausted by one-to-one coaching sessions than other coaches do. Perhaps since you became a coach, you have found yourself missing the companionship and the buzz of working in an organization. It could be that you have experience as a trainer or facilitator and want to maintain that aspect of your work. If some of this resonates with you, I encourage you to consider offering group coaching.

In all group coaching programmes, I teach some basic coaching principles so that the group members feel confident to coach one another, using the models presented to them throughout the programme.

Elements of a Group Coaching Programme

I think group coaching is something of a hybrid. It sits somewhere between one-to-one coaching, group facilitation, a support group meeting and a personal development workshop.

The following are some of the core elements I include when I am running group coaching programmes.

Contracting

It goes without saying that contracting with the group is paramount. The contract needs to cover not only confidentiality and ground rules but 'What sort of group do we want to be?' and 'What changes do we want to have achieved by the final session?', along with 'How will we each let the group know if we need some help?' and 'How shall we respond if a group member is upset?' Individual group members let the whole group know 'what I need from this group to feel like I can be myself here'.

Speaking positively about personal successes, strengths and achievements

In the first session and regularly throughout the programme, members share with the whole group their successes, strengths, progress, key achievements, things they are proud of and things they like about themselves. They also share with the group their hopes, dreams and goals and all group members make commitments to actions at the end of each group coaching session.

Different learning styles

Everyone has different preferences and learning styles, and when you are delivering group coaching, it is important to use different methods of delivery to accommodate the range of learning styles in the group. Changing the pace and style of the session also keeps group members alert and interested. You could incorporate poems, stories and metaphors with the group, or build in creative approaches such as drawing or working with Play-Doh. You could get the group moving by walking and coaching outdoors.

Peer coaching

Group members can work in pairs, on their own and in the large group, often co-coaching. We regularly have a round of coaching questions, where each group member takes it in turn to present the group with something they would like help with. Then I and the other group members ask them coaching questions to move them forward in their thinking. Each member of the group has the opportunity to be coached by the whole group in this way.

Work between sessions

I often give the group members coaching work to do between sessions. It might be reading, completing a coaching exercise or sometimes asking for feedback about themselves from people in their lives. Group members also set challenges for themselves, and one another, between sessions.

Information and coaching resources

I set up a resource table in the room, and on the first session I bring books or articles for the table which I think may be of interest to the coaching group. I encourage group members to bring things for the resource table in subsequent sessions.

Offering support within the group

We have ever-present flip charts on which group members can offer support or information to the other members. I have seen people offering their services as a hairdresser, plumber, coder, a listening ear and a mentor for someone going for promotion. I've also seen group members offer help with CV writing, interview skills, how to start running or healthy eating – and one member even offered to teach the group salsa dancing.

Celebration

The final group coaching session is always a review and celebration of successes – both individual and collective. I often ask each group member to come to the final session with an object, a poem, a piece of text or music that represents for them the experience in the coaching group. Sometimes I even end by telling the group members what gift I would like to give them, just as my tutors did for me many years earlier.

Maintaining a Coaching Stance

One of the main attractions of group coaching is the word 'coaching'. Even if you are introducing coaching skills to the group, that doesn't make it a coaching experience. It could just be a workshop. A group coaching experience means that the coach models a coaching approach with the group. This requires the coach to be asking more than telling, creating an environment in which the group members work to their own agendas and providing the conditions for group members to find their own unique solutions to their specific situations. If you are coaching a group, you will need to develop the skill of quietly noticing the interpersonal dynamics of the group members, without 'diagnosing' or becoming attached to your own hypothesis about the individuals or the group. Just as you do when you are coaching on a one-to-one basis, you will need to practise noticing what is said in the group, as well as what is not said, and noticing repeating patterns of behaviour. You will need to maintain a coaching approach, which means asking coaching questions about what you have seen, heard and experienced.

The role of the coach is key when a group comes together for the first time, and it is widely accepted that the group's reliance on the group leader is highest in the beginning and gradually lessens as the group becomes an entity of its own, as Cara found in Case Study 8.3. In the first session, it is important to establish clearly the limits of confidentiality, to generate a sense of energy and excitement about the coaching work you will do together and to establish your credibility as a group coach. In groups, there is always the potential for one or two people to dominate the conversation and therefore the time. If you are running a coaching group, where a group of individuals have each paid to experience some coaching, it is very important to ensure that the same amount of time is allocated to each member of the group to explore their situation. This should be covered in the initial contracting session and reinforced at the beginning of subsequent sessions. As a facilitator of a coaching group, the issue of time management is one of the few areas in which you can adopt an authoritative approach with the group.

Just as Tom suggests in Case Study 8.2, there is a great opportunity for you to share some basic one-to-one coaching models and techniques with the group and encourage them to experience coaching one another during the session too. When a coaching group is established, it can be a delight to see the level of mutual support generated among the members.

Case Study 8.3: Cara

Cara had run a lot of personal development programmes before training as a coach. She loved working with groups and decided to combine her skills and experiences and run group coaching programmes for people who wanted more confidence. It was a winning formula for her. 'There aren't many people who think that they already have enough confidence', she always said. Her coaching groups were consistently fully booked.

In one of her groups, all the group members lacked confidence for different reasons and one of them was a shy, quiet man in his mid-forties who had never been in a relationship. During the group coaching sessions, he revealed that his dream was to meet a woman with whom he could spend the rest of his life, but he simply didn't know how to go about it and didn't have the confidence to get started. Cara didn't find out until some months later that the other members of the group had taken him on as a 'project' outside the coaching group sessions. They had even been on a shopping trip together one weekend to give him a style makeover, choosing new outfits for him, including taking him to have a haircut and choosing new glasses for him. It made Cara so happy to picture them all on this trip – a motley crew of people, all different ages and from completely different backgrounds and all of whom had low levels of self-confidence themselves, united in support of one of their group members. The group members had then helped him to write his online dating profile and coached and supported him through his first dates. In fact, all the group members grew in confidence from the experience as they had all, without exception, stepped outside their comfort zones and dared to do something new, which needed courage.

Working with a Co-Coach

Maintaining a coaching stance when working with a group of people can be challenging. It is so much easier to fall into the role of consultant or trainer, particularly if this is one of your other regular professional roles. A coaching way of working needs to be clearly contracted at the beginning of any group coaching assignment but, as group coach, you will probably need to work harder to stay in coaching mode with a group of people than you do when working on a one-to-one basis. You will also be at risk of being pulled into some of the group dynamics and unconscious processes of the group. There will inevitably be some group members you like more than others. There could be situations which trigger your own emotional hot-spots, such as seeing someone being treated unfairly or noticing coalitions forming within the group. Your own historical experiences of being in teams, groups or families will be accessed by being in a group context, and you may find yourself being emotionally 'hooked' and finding it harder to access a coaching mindset.

Ideally, a group coach's presence embodies the knowledge, practices and theories which are believed to be essential to bring about change. These include demonstrating comfort with emotions, both positive and negative, and the ability to use assertive communication skills. A group is likely to learn as much from experiencing the presence of the coach as from the other coaching interventions. Perhaps for the first time the group members will learn, by observing the coach, that feedback, conflict and praise are healthy and useful aspects of human interaction and can be experienced in an adult way. To maintain a strong coaching presence, a group coach needs to be able to recognize their own feelings and responses quickly.

One of the most effective ways of maintaining a strong coaching presence when working with a group is to work with a co-coach. This is particularly true if you are working with a large coaching group. The benefits of working with a co-coach are:

- **You can 'meta-coach' one another**. This means observing one another interacting with the group and highlighting to your co-coach each time you notice them being emotionally hooked by something that happens. Perhaps you will notice your co-coach demonstrating a bias towards certain members of the group and you can point this out. You can provide one another with both support and challenge.
- **You can sense check your hunches**. For example, you might check in with your co-coach in the following way: 'Am I right in thinking that the group is behaving in a hostile way towards Debbie or am I imagining it?'
- **You can keep each other energized**. If one of you finds that your energy is flagging, your co-coach can step up their energy levels to give the other one time to recharge. Group coaching can be a physically and emotionally tiring business.
- **You can share observations**. With a large group of people, it is difficult for one person to observe everything that is happening. Two coaches will see and hear more than one coach working alone.

Group Coaching in Organizations

Case Study 8.4: Ella

Ella decided to start a family when she was in her mid-forties, after a long and successful career as a director in an international company. Becoming a parent made Ella aware of the competing demands involved in being a parent as well as holding down a job. She felt guilty that she hadn't ever appreciated the stresses which some of her direct reports had been managing. When Ella retrained as a coach, she decided that she wanted to develop a group coaching programme for parents in organizations. The focus of the group coaching sessions would be for the parents to acquire some coaching skills which they could use in their family life and, at the same time, have some mutual support. Ella persuaded her previous employer to let her run some pilot coaching groups for parents so that she could test the idea and get some feedback and testimonials she could use in her marketing. From the outset, there were waiting lists of eager employees wanting to attend the group coaching sessions. Ella ran six coaching groups in the first year.

The feedback from the delegates and the organization revealed an exciting and unexpected benefit of the group coaching sessions. The people who had attended the group coaching sessions had seamlessly and unknowingly started using coaching approaches with their teams. Members of the parent coaching groups had absorbed, understood and implemented coaching approaches back in the workplace with their teams far more effectively than those who had attended coaching skills for managers training programmes. This was an interesting development because there was no expectation for them to use the coaching skills back in the workplace. Ella and the members of her coaching groups for parents believed that, by fully understanding and experiencing the benefits of coaching for themselves in a different context, they were completely convinced of the benefits of coaching at work too. The organization saw this as an important move towards creating a coaching culture in the organization, and they concluded that people were more likely to engage with learning if it had relevance to them personally and they did not feel that they were being told how to use it.

External one-to-one coaching tends to be reserved for senior managers and directors in most organizations because the financial investment is considered too high for it to be made widely available in the organization. There are some notable exceptions when one-to-one coaching is used for a more junior member of staff, usually because there is a specific presenting issue which cannot be addressed via training, occupational health or employee assistance programmes. Junior or middle managers in organizations often don't have access to external coaching but may have access to coaching from internal coaches or receive coaching from their line manager.

Group coaching is now opening up as a potential new offering in organizations. Group coaching is affordable and scalable for organizations as it enables several people to be coached at the same time. It can be delivered virtually or in person, and group members may be from different parts of the organization. Bringing employees together in a coaching group can increase cross-functional understanding and collaboration. The sharing of experiences, resources, support and challenge can be as important to the group as the interventions from the coach. Strong relationships established between coaching group members can develop and grow a network of support across the organization. Group members may start to use the coaching approaches they have experienced with their teams and throughout the wider business, as we saw with Ella in Case Study 8.4.

If you are considering offering some group coaching in organizations, it may be worth approaching special interest groups within the organization, for instance, Family Network, or LGBT (lesbian, gay, bisexual and transgender) networks, as Ella did.

Coaching Exercises

This is a reflection exercise which you can use on your own, as a journaling activity or in a co-coaching session. You can use the exercise if you are thinking about developing a group or team coaching offering. It will enable you to identify emotions, situations or people who could potentially derail you from being at your best in a team or group coaching situation. It will also help you to highlight areas for development or topics to take to your own coaching or coaching supervision sessions.

Reflection questions for team or group coaches

- What positive experiences have I had in a team or group?
- What negative experiences have I had in a team or group?
- What assumptions about teams or groups do I bring to my work as a coach?
- What role(s) do I tend to assume when I am in a team or group?
- Which behaviours in others are likely to evoke in me positive feelings?
- Which behaviours in others are likely to evoke in me negative feelings?
- When was the last time I got 'rattled' by someone and what rattled me?
- What happened to my ability to choose my behaviour when I was rattled?

Twelve prerequisites for group or team coaching

If you are a new coach and want to explore your readiness for coaching a group or a team, Table 8.1 is a useful checklist for you to go through. Mark yourself between 1 and 10 for each category to identify which are areas of strength and experience for you and which areas indicate that you need more experience, skills, training or knowledge.

Table 8.1 Prerequisites for group or team coaching

One-to-one coaching experience/qualifications	Strong boundary management	Experience/training/ qualifications in working with groups or teams
Understanding of or training in team/group dynamics	High levels of self-awareness	Ability to communicate assertively
A structured team coaching process in place	Knowledge of or training in team diagnostic models	Understanding of your own relationship with conflict
Credibility with your target client group(s)	Experience of co-coaching	Regular supervision for your coaching practice

Suggested Further Reading

Britton, J.J. (2011) *Effective Group Coaching, Tried and Tested Tools and Resources for Optimum Coaching Results.* Mississauga, Canada: John Wiley & Sons Canada Ltd.

Rogers, J. (2007) *Adults Learning*, 5th edn. Maidenhead: Open University Press.

Thornton, T. (2010) *Group and Team Coaching (Essential Coaching Skills and Knowledge)*. Hove: Routledge.

9 Coaching Dilemmas

The more you coach, the more likely it is that you will encounter questions and dilemmas about coaching and about situations with your clients which had not occurred to you before. This chapter will explore some of the dilemmas and questions frequently brought to me by newly qualified coaches. If you have considered what you might do in certain situations before they arise, you will probably be better equipped to deal with them if they do happen to you. But it is worth remembering that sometimes when you encounter a difficult situation in real life, you can find yourself responding to it quite differently from when it was just a hypothetical exercise.

Coaching Conundrums

I am constantly surprised by the stories coaches tell me about the issues they face. Here are some of the more frequently asked questions:

- What do I do if my client is resistant to being coached?
- How much should I chase a client who cancels appointments?
- What if my client is already seeing another coach or therapist?
- A lot of my clients decide to leave their organization after having had coaching. I don't feel good about this if the organization has paid me to coach them. How do I handle it?
- What do I do if I think an organization is trying to get rid of my client, but my client does not realize?

This is by no means an exhaustive list of coaching conundrums. Together they serve as a reminder of how important it is to contract clearly, maintain your own boundaries and make sure you have support and supervision (see Case Study 9.1).

> **Case Study 9.1: Sarah**
>
> Sarah had a history of struggling with a people-pleasing tendency and believed that she had it under control by the time she embarked on her

new career as a coach. Her first client was a young single mother. She had no family nearby and no support with her children. She lacked confidence and wanted to use coaching to find out how she could get some time for herself. After three coaching sessions, Sarah did not feel that they had made any progress and she found herself spontaneously offering to babysit for her client to give her a break from the children. Sarah realized that her people-pleasing tendencies were still far from sorted, and she decided to enrol on an assertiveness programme.

Resistant Clients

Case Study 9.2: Peter

Peter is a relaxed person who was drawn to a non-directive coaching approach as soon as he began his coach training. He decided he would adopt this style in his coaching practice as it fitted with his non-interventionist attitude to leadership and to life in general. Peter has a firm belief that the client is a whole and fully functioning adult who does not need to be accountable to the coach. He does not set homework between coaching sessions and he does not check up on his clients' progress, even when they return for subsequent coaching sessions. He believes that his role is to create a space in which the client can think, in the presence of an empathetic and interested listener who asks them some great questions.

Peter has recently had a few clients cancel appointments at the last minute or not show up. Some clients have cancelled several appointments one after another and Peter has not seen them for some time. Peter has a cancellation policy in place in his coaching contract and has invoiced the clients, who have all paid the cancellation charge, but he is not sure how to deal with the repeated cancellations or whether he should chase his clients to rebook and complete all the sessions they signed up for.

Peter is also working with a new client who is resistant to being coached. He is on a leadership programme in his organization and all delegates on the programme have been assigned a coach for four sessions. He tells Peter that he is too busy to attend the coaching sessions and, in any case, has never seen any evidence that coaching works. During their first session, when Peter asked him questions, he had nothing to say. He told Peter that he can't see the point of coaching. Peter is unsure about how to proceed.

Some clients will have been sent to you for coaching by their organization, and, like Peter in Case Study 9.2, you may find that they are resistant to the idea. Perhaps they do not really understand what coaching is or they feel worried about opening up to a stranger. If you are an internal coach, the coachee may feel worried about confidentiality and whether, as a fellow employee in the organization, you have a covert agenda. For some people, being told that they are being given a coach can make them worry that they are doing something wrong or that their performance is in question. In this case they may also be worried that you are going to be reporting back to their boss about them. Others may feel that they do not have time for coaching and it is just adding to their workload. For some people it takes a little time to get used to the idea of coaching. These clients may struggle to come up with topics for coaching on demand. One way around this is to provide prospective clients with a list of topics that people typically discuss in coaching sessions so that they have an idea about which areas of life and work they can bring to coaching.

In organizations where coaching is established as part of the culture, it is less likely that you will encounter resistance to coaching. On the contrary, it may be seen as an accolade and be welcomed as an opportunity for career development and personal development. It is certainly an indication that the organization is prepared to invest in the employee. Even if there is a focus on improving a skill or changing a behaviour, it is probably because the organization is preparing the employee for their next role. For example, I coached someone whom the organization called 'a board director in waiting'. She had been identified as board-level material and, while waiting for a suitable role to become available, the company wanted her to have some coaching to brush up on specific skills that would be required in the new role in the areas of strategic thinking, communication and public speaking. My client was able to prepare herself for a major career transition before it happened, and I continued to coach her when she was appointed to the new role.

If you do find yourself with a resistant, sceptical or hesitant client, you need to dedicate time to allaying their fears about coaching, reassuring them about lines of reporting and confidentiality and ensuring that you contract very clearly about how you will work together. This is an even more important conversation for internal coaches to have with coachees who struggle to believe that the coaching conversations will be confidential. The topic of confidentiality should be revisited whenever you feel any new resistance. Similar conversations can also take place during chemistry sessions with the client and in three-way meetings between you, the coachee and the person from the organization who is sponsoring the coaching. There is more about how to manage chemistry sessions and three-way conversations in Chapter 4.

I often remind reluctant clients that their organization is paying a lot of money for my services, which means the organization is investing in them because they value them and want to support their development. I also mention that many people seek out coaching and pay for it themselves, if their organization is not prepared to fund it for them, because they consider it such an important contributor to their career success and personal growth.

Resistance from a client is data for you and for the client. Resistance is something that can be addressed openly in coaching sessions and you can explore together what underlies it. It may be straightforward resistance to change. Change is hard because we like familiarity. Our neurophysiology keeps us doing the same things, even when they are not helpful to us. As coaches, we need to approach change carefully and explore the costs and benefits of making changes and how a change will affect our wider system, such as other people in our lives. Helping clients to make positive changes in their lives is what you do as a coach. Exploring a client's resistance to coaching can lead to a wider exploration of the client's resistance in other areas of their life.

There are many factors stopping people from making the changes they say they want to make: fear, money, resources, confidence, skill, other people, beliefs and assumptions, time, habit, inertia, conditioning – to name only a few. A good coach will explore all these obstacles with their clients to uncover their resistance to change. The same approach can be used to uncover resistance to coaching itself. A good coach will build trust and rapport with a resistant client and work with ease, not urgency or more resistance. If all this fails and your client remains permanently resistant to the coaching process or to your style of coaching, you will need to give both your client and their organization the option of stopping the sessions. A final three-way session would give you all the opportunity to create a respectful ending and leave the door open for further sessions if the client wanted to come back.

Encountering resistance from a self-nominated and self-funding client is a different matter. Generally, when someone has decided to invest in coaching for themselves, they are ready for the work and open to the challenge before it has even started. Therefore, resistance in clients who have chosen to have coaching may have different underlying causes. A client may be experiencing high levels of stress and have decided to get some coaching. This may mean that strong emotions have hijacked their thinking and they find themselves unable to think rationally, objectively or strategically. As a coach you will be used to encouraging clients to reflect, plan, consider their options, take an objective view of their situation, receive feedback and set some goals for the future. If your client is incapable of doing these things and responds to you with black and white thinking or lots of 'I don't know' responses, they may be in survival mode. You will need to help your client back into competency mode before the coaching can begin. You can do this by creating a safe space and listening to the client with empathy and unconditional positive regard until the client is ready to start thinking about moving forward. You might also suggest that some form of counselling, such as cognitive behavioural therapy, could help them to deal with their stress or anxiety and then they could return for coaching when the counselling has brought them to a more resourceful place.

It could be that you are moving the client too quickly, and instead of telling you this directly, they are displaying resistance to the process. Whatever the cause, the resistance can be a starting point for an open and supportive conversation that might lead both of you to a clearer understanding of the client's state of mind. The following questions could help:

- What could I (the coach) do differently?
- What do you fear might happen in the coaching sessions?

- What would be the best outcome from the coaching sessions for you?
- What will help you to feel safe and in control here?
- What support do you want from me to help you to engage in the coaching process?
- How does your response to the coaching reflect your response in other areas of your life?
- If you absolutely knew that you had control of this process, how would you be and what would you do?

Dealing with Cancellations, No-Shows and Unfinished Coaching Assignments

Last-minute cancellations happen to all of us from time to time – it's normal life. However, some clients cancel repeatedly, and others fail to complete the coaching sessions they signed up for.

It is important to have a clear cancellation policy in place and to make your clients explicitly aware of the policy in your initial contracting sessions. If you have a cancellation policy and the client is aware of it, you can then make a discretionary judgement about whether to enforce it, depending on the circumstances. For example, in my practice, I would probably waive the cancellation fee for a first appointment and let the client know that there should have been a charge but it has been waived. This will also gently remind the client that there is a cancellation policy in place for future missed appointments. I would also waive the fee in the case of a real emergency for the client. But I would not waive the fee for a client who repeatedly cancelled. This is a judgement that only you can make. One of my clients has a demanding job and travels around the world at short notice. We secure dates in the diary for future coaching sessions, but she usually cancels on the day of the planned session. My client is always very apologetic and assures me that it's no problem for her organization to pay for the cancelled sessions. I am uncomfortable about wasting the company's money, my client's lack of commitment to the coaching work and the unsatisfactory nature of seeing a client so sporadically. I have recently communicated my thoughts to my client and the organization (in a coaching style, of course) and they have both agreed that we should postpone our coaching sessions until the client is in a position to make a regular commitment to her development.

Another question is whether, or for how long, you chase a client who has not completed all their sessions with you and who has regularly cancelled sessions. I would always suggest following up initially with a client to ask their reasons for not continuing. If the client does not reply the first time, one further contact from you is probably enough before you back off. As a coach, it is important for you to continue to model an open and honest communication style, which means asking direct questions, rather than making assumptions, attempting to read your client's mind or avoiding difficult conversations altogether.

There are many reasons that clients stop attending their sessions. Sometimes they get what they need in the first couple of sessions and cannot see the point in returning for more. Some clients will explain this to their coach. Others drift away without ever giving a reason. Some clients are disappointed in the coaching and, perhaps out of politeness, keep that to themselves. But it may not be about the coaching. Sometimes, your client's behaviour with you is representative of how they behave generally. If you suspect this is the case, it is worth letting your client know how you experience them to see if that brings any new insights.

One of my clients entered into his coaching sessions with real enthusiasm, but by the third session his enthusiasm had started to wane. I said to him, 'I get the sense that you are not as enthusiastic about the coaching as you were before' and he acknowledged that this was the case. I asked what I could do differently to rekindle his enthusiasm and he didn't know. I asked, 'I wonder if this is a pattern for you. Are there other areas of your life where you have lost interest in something quickly?' This conversation led to some real breakthrough moments in our relationship and in his self-awareness.

I believe an essential role for coaches is to hold up the mirror to their clients and to draw their attention to the way in which you experience them. We need to be courageous enough to share our hunches, intuitions and feelings with the client and to present them as musings, not finite truths. We need to ask the question implicitly, and sometimes explicitly: 'Is this about me and my stuff or about you and your stuff?' Some useful introductory phrases to use are: 'I am wondering . . .', 'I get the sense that . . .', 'I am feeling . . .', 'My mind is thinking . . .', 'What I receive from you is . . .'.

If your clients regularly cancel, this is an issue worth taking to coaching supervision. It could be that your contracting is not clear or that your boundaries are loose. It could be that you are not reading early warning signals from your clients or not giving your clients the opportunity to tell you what is working or not working for them in your coaching sessions . . . or you could just be unlucky. Either way, it is your responsibility to notice repeating patterns in your own coaching work and try to work out if you are contributing to them in any way (see Case Study 9.3).

Case Study 9.3: Colin

Colin noticed that lots of his coaching clients didn't complete all their coaching sessions with him. They typically cancelled after the first two or three sessions and often didn't make contact with him again. Colin suspected that he went too quickly into deep, personal issues and scared his clients off.

He discussed this with his supervisor and identified that he had always wanted to be a psychotherapist but had become a coach because the training was shorter and less intensive. Colin identified a few options: 1. train as a therapist; 2. change his behaviour of going quickly into psychological territory in coaching relationships; 3. be explicit with prospective clients about his 'deep' coaching approach.

By taking notice of a repeating pattern in his clients' response to him, Colin was able to develop a new way forward. He decided to train as a therapist, while continuing to work as a coach but managing his tendency to teeter into therapeutic territory in coaching relationships. His clients stopped cancelling and Colin is feeling excited about being able to offer therapy as well as coaching in the future.

Coaching Someone who is Already Working with a Coach or Therapist

I was once coaching a client as part of an organizational brief and felt resistance from him. When I mentioned this to him in the second session, he told me that he had his own personal coach and did not want the work that we were doing together to compromise any of the work he was doing with his own coach. When I take on clients who are paying for themselves, I always ask, along with my other intake questions, whether they are seeing another coach or a therapist. I had not done the same for my clients in a corporate setting until this situation arose, and since then I have routinely asked the question of all my coaching clients.

What do you do if a client is seeing another coach or therapist? First, talk to them about what objectives they are working on with the other coach and why they feel the need to engage an additional helping professional. I have clients who also see a style coach or a voice coach and so there is no conflict of interest with work they might do with me. In other instances, the work they are doing with someone else seems very close to the work we are proposing to do together. In both cases, it is essential that the client speaks to their existing coach or therapist to check with them whether they foresee any conflict of interest if the client begins to work with me, even if there is a different focus to the sessions. I do not start working with a client until everyone involved agrees that there is no conflict.

Who is my Client – the Organization or the Coachee?

If you are a coach working in organizations, you will almost certainly find yourself asking: who is the client? Is it the organization that is paying for the coaching, or is it the person sitting in the chair in front of you? Actually, both are your clients. You want to do a good job for the individual and for the company. You have a commercial relationship with the organization, which you hope will continue, and you have a personal relationship with the individual, which will probably become stronger as you get to know them in your coaching sessions.

Considering both parties to be your clients does not pose any problems until it transpires that they want different outcomes from the coaching or if the people you coach are leaving their organizations in droves. It also becomes difficult if you think that your client would be better off leaving the organization or if you have a sneaking suspicion that the organization would prefer your client to leave.

To avoid the potential for dilemmas or conflicts of this nature, it is important to highlight the situations which could occur, before the coaching has started, in contracting sessions with the organization. I always say to the sponsor of the coaching that sometimes people leave the organization after having been coached. Some people do this without ever mentioning their intentions to the coach. Others do tell the coach that they are thinking of leaving the organization. I also stress that these are relatively rare occurrences. Having this conversation in advance is important and gives you and the corporate sponsor an opportunity to discuss how you would deal with these situations in terms of roles, processes, expectations and confidentiality.

In my experience, most organizations accept that an employee leaving the company is a potential outcome of any coaching intervention. Most organizations also say that they genuinely want what is best for the person and that having an unhappy employee does not benefit anyone.

Sometimes organizations have said to me before the coaching has started that they want me to ensure that their employee does not leave the organization. I am always clear that I cannot give this guarantee. I do reassure them, however, that I have both the organization's and the coachee's interests in mind at all times and that coaching is as likely to support the employee in staying with the company, where that would benefit both parties, as to facilitate the employee's departure.

If your coachee discloses to you that they are unhappy and thinking of leaving the organization, you will no doubt approach this from a coaching perspective by listening, questioning, challenging, raising awareness, changing perspective and all the other coaching techniques you use. In addition to taking a pure coaching approach, it is wise to talk to your coachee about your role in this, speaking openly about any conflict you are experiencing and how you manage your contract with both the coachee and the organization. This will include reminding the coachee of the confidentiality arrangements which were agreed at the initial three-way meeting.

As always, talking to a coaching supervisor about this kind of dilemma is essential for you to get clarity about the way forward and some necessary reassurance about responsibility. Coaches often take a lot of responsibility for decisions their coachees make, particularly if they do not benefit the organization. A supervisor will help you to think through where the responsibility lies.

If you have found yourself in a situation where a number of your coachees have left an organization and the organization has not followed up with you, you should follow up with them. Once again, you will be demonstrating coaching behaviours: open and honest communication and dealing with difficult situations in an adult way. A conversation with the corporate sponsor about what has happened and whether either you or the organization can gain any insights from the situation could be valuable for both of you. The organization will also respect your concern for them and your integrity about your work as a coach.

How do I Know if There is a Hidden Agenda?

Jason has been offering personal coaching for two years and has recently secured his first corporate coaching assignments. He admits, on reflection, that he did not contract effectively with the organization and he did not manage his boundaries well. The corporate sponsor made a number of throwaway comments in the initial phone call to Jason to the effect that they wouldn't mind if the employee left the business as a result of the coaching sessions. Because Jason was not experienced or confident about managing a three-way contract, he did not pick up on these comments at the time. Since he has started coaching the employee, he has learned that the organization has demoted him, reduced his workload so that he is doing basic administrative duties and moved his desk from the main office into a side room.

Jason has been working with the client on building his confidence and developing his skills so that he will be more appreciated by his employers. Although Jason's client has made positive changes, they have not been noticed by his employers and it appears as though he is being increasingly sidelined. It has not crossed the client's mind that his job might be at risk. Weighing up all the evidence, Jason now feels that the organization is trying to make his client's situation so difficult that he will resign. Jason does not know what he should do. Should he speak to the organization or to his client about his fears, or do nothing and keep coaching the client on building his confidence?

There are a number of ways in which coaches can be involved with employees who are leaving organizations. Some companies offer two or three coaching sessions for employees who are leaving to provide support for them during the transition. This is usually only available to senior employees where the company has initiated their exit. It can take the form of outplacement coaching or it can be simply a way of offering the exiting employee general coaching support. There is also a growing trend for specialist 'exit coaches'. Exit coaches typically work with CEOs or chairs of businesses on planning their exit strategy and, depending on circumstances, these coaches may also be involved in supporting the sale of the business. Either way, the coach should be engaged transparently. In Case Study 9.4, there was no open discussion with Jason, just some asides from the corporate sponsor. This would pose a dilemma for any coach. First, how does Jason know that his hunch is correct? How can he find out? Does he need to find out? What is Jason's role in this? What has he been engaged to do? Where does his loyalty lie – to the person he is coaching or to the organization? Jason is not an employment lawyer or HR specialist and he knows nothing about this area anyway so what does he propose to do about it? He is not a consultant and his role is not to give advice. Where does this leave him?

There is no single right answer to this dilemma. As with all coaching assignments, the contracting session is key. In the contracting session, a coach will explain the boundaries of coaching, the parameters of confidentiality, feedback mechanisms and associated confidentiality boundaries. With hindsight, Jason should have questioned the throwaway comments and been clear with the sponsor that a coach's role is not to support an employee's exit unless this has been transparently agreed by all three parties.

If the contracting session has not been effectively managed, the coach might be faced later on with an ethical decision about how to deal with a situation of this kind. The options open to the coach are:

- **Just keep coaching the client**. Rely on good coaching questions to raise the client's awareness. Use exercises which encourage perspective shift, such as 'What would you say/think if you were looking in on your work situation?' or 'What do you think your boss is thinking now?'
- **Remember that you are not a consultant or an advisor**. Remember that you are not responsible for the outcome. Revisit your code of practice and ethical guidelines and consult your supervisor for guidance.
- **Have open conversations with the client and the corporate sponsor in which you share your concerns**. Be prepared to end the coaching sessions if you feel that you are too compromised to carry on.

Do I Need a List of Other People to Whom I can Refer my Clients?

Case Study 9.5: Valentina

Valentina specializes in coaching senior leaders who want to increase their executive presence and gravitas. She has no training in this, so she offers to introduce her clients to an image consultant. Valentina has every confidence in the image consultant's knowledge, professionalism and confidentiality. She has known her for years. Valentina receives no referral fee for the introduction. The image consultant, in turn, often refers her clients to Valentina for coaching. This mutually beneficial relationship comes from the trust and respect they have for each other's high professional standards and a clear agreement about how they will manage referrals.

It can be useful to have a network of people whose professional services you know, respect and trust – for example, a therapist, financial advisor, style consultant, voice coach, personal trainer, lawyer – but there are a few caveats to making referrals.

Referrals to third parties must be done in accordance with your professional code of ethics, which means that you will need to disclose to your client and the sponsor(s) any anticipated compensation from the third parties that you may receive for the referral. Any referrals should come about because your client asks you if you know anyone who could provide those services and not because you prescribe these services to your client. Ensure that the boundaries are clear between the work you are doing with your client and work that any third party might do with them. You need to be confident that you have personal experience of any third parties you are referring your clients to and that you genuinely believe they offer a good service, have full professional insurance and operate with integrity (see Case Study 9.5).

Do I Accept my Client's Version of Reality or do I Collect External Feedback?

Case Study 9.6: Derek

Derek is an experienced coach who has been coaching the CEO of a business for about a year. The CEO's goal for coaching was to improve his relationship with his financial director (FD). The CEO felt that he was being excessively judgemental and negative about the FD because the FD 'wasn't his type of person'. The CEO said that other members of the board and others in the business seemed to respect and value the FD. So Derek had coached the CEO over a number of sessions to increase his client's empathy and tolerance towards his FD. Some months after the coaching sessions had ended, Derek by chance met the FD concerned at a business networking event. Derek was shocked. He experienced the FD as difficult and belligerent.

The experience troubled Derek greatly. He had accepted the CEO's version of the situation and had spent several coaching sessions trying to increase the CEO's compassion and understanding. Derek wondered how he would have approached the coaching sessions if he had met the FD before starting to coach the CEO. Now a new client has asked Derek to accompany him to a meeting at work. In the light of his earlier experience, Derek thinks this could be helpful in giving him a grasp of the reality of the situation, but he is not sure whether this is really part of his role as a coach.

From time to time clients may ask you to observe them in their workplace. Most commonly a client will ask you to attend a meeting which the client is going to be running. Usually clients will make this request because they have received adverse comment on their leadership style and they are looking for additional and objective feedback, or it may be because they have been working on their leadership style in the coaching sessions and want feedback to help them measure their progress. Any departures from the traditional coaching arrangement should be carefully contracted, including contracting with anyone else who is going to be involved. You would need to think about who else is going to be in the meeting and how you should contract with them. However, sometimes moving outside the coaching room in a considered way can be helpful in challenging a coach's perceptions or assumptions, as Derek discovered when he met his client's FD (in Case Study 9.6). Sometimes a coach offering support in the 'real' environment can provide a moment of powerful affirmation to a client.

Whether coaches should coach only in the 'bubble' of the coaching room is an open question, along with how far you can rely on your client's version of reality. You will only get your client's perspective, because that is all they can give you. The role of the coach is to hear how the client represents their perspective or their 'reality' and to notice not just what they say but how they say it. To be aware of what they choose to focus on and what they omit. The coach's role is to notice repeating patterns in the client's psychology over time. Do they always feel let down by people, or are they describing an isolated incident? You will need to wait, withhold judgement and keep any hypotheses parked somewhere in the back of your mind until you have enough evidence, before raising such a pattern and exploring it with your client.

Many coaches work exclusively in the 'here and now' with their clients, attending only to the issues the client presents to them and relying on their own responses to the client. Other coaches use a range of approaches to help them gain perspective and external feedback on the client's situation. These may include observing the client in their role at work and attending meetings with the client's line managers or peers, either by themselves or in a triad format. They may also use diagnostic tests, psychometric assessments and 360-degree feedback questionnaires.

Some organizational briefs for coaching assignments insist that part of the assignment includes using a diagnostic framework, psychometric test or 360-degree appraisal. If you are not qualified in any psychometric test, you may decide to get some additional training in a personality profiling tool of your choice, particularly if you are working in organizations that are looking for external coaches to provide profiling as part of the coaching assignment. Requests for coaching assignments by organizations are often prompted by the results of an internal appraisal or feedback system, so it is helpful for you to be aware of the tool that the company uses, even if you are not qualified to deliver it.

360-degree feedback

You may also choose to gather external feedback on your client as this can provide invaluable perspective on how they are seen by other people. This should, of course, always be contracted with the client and carried out with their agreement and involvement.

I have noticed that an increasing number of our corporate clients have an expectation that any executive coaching programme will include a 360-degree feedback exercise on the coachee. 360-degree feedback, as the name suggests, involves asking for feedback about the coachee from a range of people in the coachee's work life, home life or both. Usually the respondents include the coachee's boss or people they report to, the coachee's direct reports, peers, clients, and sometimes even family members. Most executive coaches in my network include a 360-degree feedback exercise as a routine part of their coaching programme. However, some coach training programmes do not cover 360-degree feedback and it can be a surprise to new coaches to find themselves being asked for this service. 'How do I run a 360?' is a question which often crops up in supervision sessions or on discussion forums for coaches. There is no one way in which to do it. How you go about it depends on time, budget, organizational requirements and perhaps the coach's preferences too. There are a number of 'off the shelf' online 360-degree diagnostics on the market. My personal preference is for bespoke feedback, tailored to meet the requirements of the coachee, the client, the reason for the coaching assignment and the goals of the coaching. If you are going to conduct 360-degree feedback, here are some aspects to consider:

How to choose who gives feedback

This is usually decided by the coachee – you ask them to choose six or eight people from different areas of the business, or from their personal life, whose opinions they trust and respect and who represent people from all around them, at different levels in the business. Occasionally, the organization will have input into this decision too.

How is the feedback gathered and by whom?

I, and most coaches in my network, conduct telephone interviews with the respondents. I schedule a 30–45-minute call with each of them and ask each one the same set of questions. I capture their answers verbatim as we are speaking. I try not to deviate into tangential conversations or topics unless they have significant relevance. Afterwards I collate all the answers in a report. Because every participant answers the same questions, it is easy to draw out themes, frequently repeated words or phrases to describe the coachee or their behaviour, and to notice differences.

Another option is for the coachee to meet the participants face to face or by phone to ask them the questions. I don't favour this option as it is more difficult for the coachee to remain objective in the conversations and perhaps more difficult for the respondents to give truly honest feedback.

Sometimes coachees email the list of questions to the participants instead of speaking directly to them. This can provide a level of detachment so that the respondent is able to be more honest.

What questions to ask

Questions should be open questions, delivered in a coaching style. 360-degree feedback works best if the questions are short and uncomplicated. When you are asking for responses to the feedback, encourage the respondents to be honest and, most importantly, to give specific examples and evidence to back up their responses.

Here are some suggestions, written as if the coachee was asking for feedback from the participants:

- What do you consider to be my greatest strengths?
- What do you consider to be my greatest achievement?
- What one word or phrase sums me up?
- What one change could I make for my own benefit?
- What one change could I make which would improve my relationship with you?
- If you could give me a piece of advice, or wisdom, what would it be?
- What wish do you have for me?
- Describe a time when you have seen me at my best. What behaviours did I exhibit?
- Describe a time when you have seen me not at my best. What behaviours did I exhibit?

Where to position the 360 in a coaching assignment

In a six-session coaching programme, it is common practice to position the 360-degree feedback around session 2 or 3. Often feedback is collected after session 2 and session 3 is dedicated to debriefing the feedback.

At this stage the coaching relationship should be established enough for the debriefing conversation to take place, with all the potential emotion, honesty and challenge it can bring.

How to debrief the feedback

An executive coach I know begins every debriefing session by asking the questions, 'What do you think were the key themes of the feedback about you? What do you think your boss/peers/direct reports said in response to the questions?' He tells me that, for the most part, his coachees' 'guesses' accurately reflect the responses. If there is a strong mismatch between the coachee's self-image and the views of the respondents, this is an area for exploration in the coaching session.

Other ways of debriefing are to share the written documents with the coachee and ask coaching questions, such as:

- What do you notice?
- What surprises you?

- How do you feel?
- Where do you agree/disagree?

Usually the debriefing conversation is powerful and emotionally charged for coachees. They often find it humbling that people have taken the time and trouble to think about them so deeply and coachees can be surprised and delighted to find out that they are held in high regard for the qualities that they themselves value.

There can be great value in the thematic nature of this feedback, in that it can be hard to ignore the same theme emerging from everyone around the coachee. However, if you find yourself wondering, like Derek in Case Study 9.6, whether you have been too ready to believe your client's version of events, then gathering external feedback is not the only solution. Fundamentally, coaching is about creating a safe, confidential space in which your client can think out loud, be understood, challenged and supported to do new things, or to do old things differently. It is a bespoke personal development journey and one of great privilege for both parties. Remember that you are experiencing the client for yourself. How do you feel when you are with them, and how likely is it that other people have the same response? This is all useful data for you. By asking the right questions, and with the help of other coaching techniques, you will be able to challenge your client's perspective and their 'take' on things and create new awareness and new possibilities.

Ideally, in a relationship of unconditional positive regard, your client can feel free to drop the need for any games, rackets or defensive strategies which they have come to rely on (see Case Study 9.7).

Case Study 9.7: Stella

Stella had coached Geoff for nearly a year. He was managing director of a small local engineering company. Stella had conducted a 360-degree feedback exercise on Geoff but had found it ineffective. Most of the responses were bland pleasantries about Geoff. He was not particularly interested in finding out what others had to say about him either. Geoff talked endlessly in the coaching sessions about his achievements, his success and how much money he was making. Stella experienced him as overbearing and lacking in humility. If you listened to Geoff, you could easily believe that he had everything under control. He said he went to the gym regularly and yet he was overweight, out of breath and not in good physical shape. He said he had stopped smoking, but Stella could still smell cigarette smoke on him. She didn't believe anything Geoff said. He pretended to be an advocate of coaching, but Stella felt no real commitment from Geoff. She imagined he was just doing it to boost his ego and show off about having a coach.

Stella spent a lot of time discussing Geoff in supervision. She asked herself, 'Is this about me? Perhaps Geoff reminds me of someone from my past and I am transferring those feelings to Geoff?' With the help of her supervisor, she eventually told Geoff how she experienced being with him. She said she felt he was playing at the coaching and always trying to impress. She told Geoff that she accepted him as he was, as a human being, and that the purpose of the coaching was to face the parts of himself and his life that he wasn't happy about, so that he could make some changes. Stella said she felt that Geoff was afraid of appearing vulnerable and this led him to be dishonest. Stella ended by saying that she could not work with him any more unless he could be honest with her.

Geoff looked shocked, became angry and then broke down in tears. For the rest of the session, Geoff talked about his difficult childhood, his insecurities, his fear of financial ruin, the breakdown of his marriage and how he learned to put on an act so that nobody would discover 'who he really was'.

Stella's commitment to the coaching process created a breakthrough moment in their coaching relationship.

Coaching Exercise

Self-reflection for coaches: 'Me, coercive? Never'

We can be unconsciously coercive if our behaviour or personality traits create a feeling of pressure in our clients. This reflection exercise is about considering how appropriately you use any of the following coaching behaviours. These are sometimes known as sources of personal power. Power is not a frequently used term in coaching, but it is important to understand what power we have and how we use it, or unconsciously misuse it, with our clients. Power can be described as the potential ability to influence behaviour, manage resistance and compel people to do things that they would not otherwise do. Whether we like it or not, as coaches we use our power and we use it positively for the benefit of our clients. However, it is possible to inadvertently misuse our power. If you rely heavily on one or two behaviours or if you overuse any of them, they could create discomfort for your client and they may feel coerced or pressurized. Consider which of the following behaviours you use and what could be the impact of them on your clients:

- Fast-paced approach to goals and actions
- Highly achievement driven – pushing client to set bigger and better goals
- Rescuing/infantilizing your client
- Needing to be liked, admired or thanked by your clients (psychologically seductive)
- Celebratory of your client's successes – praising and high-fiving

- Very optimistic about your client's potential – 'you can do it!'
- High levels of self-disclosure and comfort with deeply emotional conversations
- Expressing yourself in an over-intellectual or too theoretical way

Suggested Further Reading

Ainsworth, E.R. (2016) *360 Degree Feedback: A Transformational Approach.* St Albans: Panama Press Ltd.

Hazler, R.J. and Barwick, N. (2001) *The Therapeutic Environment (Core Concepts in Therapy).* Maidenhead: Open University Press.

O'Neill, M.B. (2000) *Executive Coaching with Backbone and Heart: A Systems Approach to Engaging Leaders with Their Challenges.* New York: Jossey-Bass.

10   When Will I Know Enough?

This chapter addresses the use of tools, techniques and models and the danger of over-focusing on them at the expense of the coaching relationship. It will look at managing and understanding your coaching toolkit – what to use when, where and with whom – and how to use tools and techniques to complement a strong coaching relationship. It will also give you an opportunity to think through whether you need or want more coaching qualifications after completing your initial training, what the reasons are for you to do further study and what might be the right timing for you.

When Will I Have Enough Qualifications?

Learning to be a coach is a wonderful experience for most people. Delegates on coach training courses often say that the experience is life-changing. You get to work with like-minded people and sometimes they become close friends. You go through a valuable personal development experience, learning about yourself through the practice coaching sessions and self-reflection. You acquire new knowledge which comes from various fields of study, including psychology, organizational development, therapy and business. You learn about building trust, rapport and respect and what it means to really listen, and this transfers into your personal life too. And you probably leave the programme with a raft of new coaching tools which you can use with your clients.

There is almost universal agreement from delegates on coaching programmes that the experience is a rich and valuable one. Coaches differ, however, in whether they feel that the training they have undergone is enough for them or whether they want to pursue further courses of study. There have often been references to, or perhaps short sessions on, specific topics on the coach training programme: neuro-linguistic programming (NLP), mindfulness, stress management, positive psychology, use of diagnostics and psychometric tools, resilience and well-being, transactional analysis, Gestalt Coaching – to name just a few.

Some coaches are drawn to a particular topic and decide to do some further study in it straight away. Other coaches are bewildered by how much there is to know and wonder where they should start and what more do they need. The people teaching on their courses seem to know so much and have so many different quali-fications that new coaches can start to wonder whether they should study more.

Coaching Tools and Techniques

> **Case Study 10.1: Melissa**
>
> Melissa offers coaching to women who are returning to the workplace after a career break. She has always liked structure in her life and in her work and, although she enjoyed training as a coach, she struggled with not having a standard process to follow. She didn't really understand what 'dancing in the moment' meant and found it difficult to go into a practice coaching session without extensive preparation. She could never think on her feet about which technique to use for which person and for whichever topic or issue was presented. She also disliked the more theatrical, creative coaching approaches as she felt uncomfortable being coached in this way herself. Melissa is diligent, kind and caring and genuinely interested in her clients. During her training, she always received positive feedback on her warmth and her listening skills. By the time Melissa qualified as a coach, she had decided that she was going to create her own standard coaching process. She designed a six-session programme, which she followed for every client. Working in this way means that Melissa knows exactly what she is doing each time she coaches and the clients have a clear six-week structure and a good understanding in advance about what they will be doing.
>
> So far this has worked well for both Melissa and her clients. However, Melissa is concerned that she has effectively rejected many coaching tools, in selecting just six to use. She can't help wondering what her clients might be missing. She is also worried that she is being overly prescriptive and leading her clients too much. She is not sure whether to keep doing what she is doing or to try to extend her range.

'How do I know which tool or technique to use with my client? I have so many to choose from and I am still not sure which technique is suitable for which presenting issue. I also don't know if I can remember how to do all the techniques.' This is a question that I am frequently asked by qualified coaches. The straightforward answer is that your toolkit of coaching techniques should be seen as a set of concepts or approaches that can be drawn on as needed.

Creating a standard coaching process

It can be a good idea to create a six-session plan as it gives your clients clarity and enables you to articulate, on your website, in leaflets and in conversation, what you offer to prospective clients. You can even have some workbooks printed for your clients, which contain the coaching questions, models or diagrams you will be using. Some clients enjoy being given a workbook or journal that they can keep as a lasting reminder of their coaching sessions with you. The downside of having just one programme is that it may not work for everyone. Melissa, in Case Study 10.1, has a niche offering, targeted to people returning to work after a career break, and therefore it is likely that the tools she has chosen will be helpful to most of her clients. If you are considering a more general coaching offering, it would be difficult to limit a programme to specific tools.

Different clients come with different situations, histories and challenges. Each coaching assignment can take unexpected twists and turns as the coaching highlights a hitherto unacknowledged strength or obstacle for the client. Clients' lives can alter in significant ways during their coaching work with you and life may throw up some unexpected issues for them, which they will bring to the coaching sessions. If this happens, the planned programme may not be the right approach and will have to be abandoned in favour of more appropriate interventions. I know many coaches who create a folder of personally tried and tested coaching. This allows them to flex their approach to the needs of the client and their individual circumstances. If you do this, it is perfectly acceptable to refer to the folder during a coaching session. Some coaches think that they must be able to recall every coaching tool or questioning model 'in the moment', but this is not necessary. Over time, with repeated use, you will remember the techniques. In the early days of your practice, referring to your materials will not make you look as if you do not know what you are doing; rather, you will look as if you care about getting things right for your client.

You could also consider creating a matrix of tools and techniques, noting when you have used each technique to good effect and with which presenting issue. You could also make notes for yourself about potential pitfalls of each technique. This will enable you to build your repertoire and your confidence.

Playing to your preferences

We are all in danger of playing to our own preferences. We are inclined to use the tools and techniques that we like best. This usually means that you have had positive experiences with these techniques, either as a coach or a client. Or it could mean that the techniques suit your personal learning style. If you are comfortable working creatively, for example, you may shy away from more process-driven approaches, and vice versa. If you did not like or understand a technique when you were doing your training, you may unconsciously avoid it. This can be a mistake. Using unfamiliar techniques and asking different types of question will create learning opportunities for you and extend your range.

Your clients may have different preferences and learning styles from you and they may have better results with exercises that you do not favour. You will need to consider how far you go in adapting to your clients' needs. If you are doing something that you do not believe in and that does not feel authentic, you will unconsciously communicate this to your client and it will affect the client's experience. However, this can be overcome by contracting very clearly with your client and being transparent in your communication.

I once had a regular client tell me that, although she really liked working with me, she did not much like the techniques I used. She said that she had hoped to work with someone who had a more 'spiritual' approach to coaching, and it is fair to say that I have a rather down to earth approach. She said that 'to help me to understand her' she had brought along a spiritual self-help book which she held in high regard. She had identified a technique in it that she wanted to experience, and she said she would like me to do this with her. We had a lengthy conversation about whether it was appropriate for me to do it. I told my client that I did not know the exercise, that I was unfamiliar with the book and the approach and that she would be better to find someone who was trained in this methodology. She implored me to do it, as she said that she had built up trust with me. So, I agreed to do it on the basis that I would merely be reading the instructions from the book and would make no other interventions. It was the most powerful coaching session we had together. My client knew what she wanted, and I had not been giving it to her, but we did have a strong relationship of trust and honesty, which enabled us to contract to do this work together.

The Relationship is Paramount

> ### Case Study 10.2: Brian
>
> During his coach training, Brian didn't enjoy using coaching techniques involving drawing, diagrams or physical movement. He didn't feel comfortable using them when he coached others and he got no value from them as a coachee. Brian believed that coaching was about listening, questioning and setting goals. He had experimented with other approaches on his coaching course but when he set up his business he decided that he would play to his preferences and offer the kind of coaching which he believed in, and the coaching he would like to receive.
>
> Brian was very clear about the sort of coaching you would get if you signed up to being coached by him.
>
> It worked very well. Brian developed a successful coaching practice. He felt that he was always giving his best to clients because he wholeheartedly believed in his approach. He was never compromised by feeling the need to use techniques he didn't fully understand or believe in. Clients who wanted a more fluid, creative coaching approach were left in no doubt that they would not get that from Brian and were free to find a different sort of coach, who would be able to meet their needs.

When you have developed a strong coaching relationship, the tools and the techniques are only one factor in bringing about lasting positive change in your client. This is similar to what Jung refers to: 'Learn your theories as well as you can but put them aside when you touch the miracle of the living soul' (Jung 1953: 73). Tools and techniques can play an important part in a coaching programme, but there is a risk in over-focusing on the tools themselves. You will no doubt have explored this topic in depth during your coach training and there is consensus about this in counselling and coaching literature: 'A preoccupation with using techniques is seen as depersonalizing the relations' (Corey 1996).

Carl Rogers (1951: 26) also often pointed out the folly of using techniques or methods without maintaining proper attention to 'unconditional positive regard' for the client and personal self-awareness:

> The client is apt to be quick to discern when the counsellor is using a 'method', an intellectually chosen tool which he has selected for a purpose. On the other hand, the counsellor is always implementing, both in conscious and non-conscious ways, the attitudes which he holds toward the client ... Thus, a counsellor who basically does not hold the hypothesis that the person has significant capacity for integrating himself may think that he has used nondirective 'methods' and 'techniques', and proved to his own satisfaction that these techniques are unsuccessful.
>
> (Rogers 1951: 26)

The client will often be able to sense if the practitioner is relying on techniques, and may be dissatisfied that their coach is not authentically engaging with them as an individual. This can break trust between the client and the coach and perhaps even lead the client to think that they are being put through a routine process. It is important to demonstrate at all times to our clients that they themselves, their situation and presenting issues are unique.

Erik de Haan (de Haan, Culpin and Curd 2011: 22–4) has written specifically about the application of techniques in coaching:

> Specific techniques and coaching interventions appear to make much less difference than the more general, common factors – and there are even strong indications that specific interventions make no difference at all ... Although we can't demonstrate that there is one specific approach that works better than others, it **is** possible to show that commitment, faith, attachment ... to an approach ... [do] make a positive difference ... Commitment to a coaching ideology and a coaching approach, to which you gear your interventions, will contribute towards your effectiveness, provided that commitment is genuine and focused on helping the client.

A good coaching relationship, built on mutual respect, is the foundation stone of the work, along with the coaching alliance or psychological contract between coach and client. Learn the coaching tools and theories but don't be too dogmatic about them. It's a fine balance between over-reliance on techniques and working without any structure. Most of the successful coaches I know work with a commitment to a set of underpinning beliefs, values and theories which guide their practice (see Case Study 10.2).

Concepts and Principles

It is helpful to think in terms of concepts and principles, rather than merely tools and techniques. The number of coaching techniques can be overwhelming, and, like many other coaches, you may be bewildered about which specific technique to use with which presenting issue. Thinking in terms of the principles that underpin the techniques will free you from thinking you have to get every step of a particular model right. This is rarely the case if you understand more about what the technique is designed to achieve.

Diagrams, images, objects and conversational metaphors

When you use any coaching technique or approach that involves objects or symbols to represent your client, you are working with metaphors. The symbols may be household objects, pictures, pebbles, diagrams, drawings or conversational images, such as the coaching question, 'What does the path towards your goal look like?' Even familiar diagrams such as the Wheel of Life are examples of metaphor. The principle behind this is that clients can talk about the object, image or diagram more easily than they can talk about themselves directly. Talking about a third-party object provides some distance and safety and allows the client to express thoughts and ideas that they may not otherwise express. Clients can feel less psychologically guarded because they are talking about the object, and not about themselves.

Working with metaphor, clients can give you and themselves a lot of information. If a client says, 'The path to my goal is blocked by immovable boulders and even if I could move them there are man-eating tigers on the other side of the boulders', you can quickly learn a lot about the client. Working with metaphor can capture the essence of someone's situation or emotions in a way that lengthy questioning sessions may not. Metaphorical ways of working also allow clients to describe difficult or emotional situations with a degree of detachment. Carl Jung (1933), one of the influential thinkers in the early days of therapy, suggested that metaphors connect with our unconscious minds, accessing thoughts and feelings that we have blocked or hidden from our conscious awareness. Metaphors can bypass our conscious minds, creating access to feelings and a deeper understanding of ourselves.

Metaphors are common in everyday language and you will probably have learned, when training to be a coach, to listen out for the metaphors your client uses, to pick up on them and to use them as you respond. Key points about other people's metaphors are that they are personal and the meaning of someone's metaphor is unique to them. Be careful not to contaminate them with your own interpretations or adaptations. Stay with your client's exact words and ask them to explain more about what meaning the metaphor has for them.

Any techniques that involve talking about oneself via an image, metaphor, diagram or object can be useful in the early stages of the coaching relationship to help clients to talk about themselves and their situation with a degree of distance and relative ease. They can also be useful at any point in the coaching relationship to enable clients to talk about more difficult thoughts, feelings or situations or to access more creative solutions to their situations.

Changing perspective

There is another useful set of techniques that involve changing perspective. The principle behind this is that we can see things more objectively when they don't apply to ourselves. Standing outside of our own viewpoint enables us to see a wider picture. We are more emotionally engaged when we are seeing things from our own perspective and more detached and dispassionate when we look at something from afar.

In coaching, perspective change can occur conversationally in response to a coaching question such as, 'What would you advise someone else to do if they were in your situation?' You could also create a more physical experience by asking a client to position themselves as if standing in another person's shoes and seeing themselves and their current situation through different eyes. I sometimes ask my client if I can pretend to be them for a moment, so that they can see how they might come across to others. I often do this if my client is minimizing their achievements or discounting their successes. One of my clients was a board-level director in a fast-growing technology company. She competed in triathlons at national level and had a high ranking in the sport. Whenever she spoke to me about her achievements, she slumped in her chair, shrugged her shoulders and said things like 'Anyone could do it. I'm nothing special. I just work hard.'

When I imitated her (and I did exaggerate it a little) she burst out laughing. She was shocked to experience the impact of such overdone modesty and realized that she could afford to speak more positively about her achievements without appearing arrogant.

Techniques involving perspective shift are useful if a client cannot generate any options and is stuck in their own set of perceptions. Using the principle of dissociation (moving away from your own perspective) can also defuse negative emotions. Conversely, using the principle of association (being fully immersed in an experience, standing in your own shoes, seeing with your own eyes) can be used to embed positive feelings and emotions. When your client is feeling great about something, encourage them to take time to experience that feeling, so that they claim it as their own and remember it.

Acting 'as if'

The psychologist Alfred Adler (1870–1937) is believed to have developed the acting 'as if' technique in psychotherapy. The technique is now widely used in coaching, therapy and personal development.

In a coaching session, you can ask your clients to act, for example, as if they were the kind of leader they want to be or the public speaker they dream of being, or to act as if they don't have the limiting beliefs about themselves that are currently holding them back. You can encourage them to act as if they had already achieved their goals or were living the life they have dreamed of. You can also ask your client to imagine an ideal version of themselves, standing in front of them. You can invite them to notice what is different from their 'real' self and then, if the client is willing, invite them to step into the shoes of their ideal self and speak, behave, think and feel from that new perspective. You can ask them, in their 'as if' persona, to give some advice or encouragement to their 'real' self.

A variation on acting 'as if' in a coaching session is to think of someone who would be very capable of doing what the client wants to do, and then pretending to be that person. This is like 'method acting', the pretend play you enjoyed when you were a child. What is remarkable about acting 'as if' techniques is that clients are usually able to assume the new behaviours quite easily. Acting 'as if' gives clients the confidence to realize that they can do it, that they already have those behaviours in their repertoire. Perhaps they have just not exercised them very much. As with the other coaching principles, this one can be applied conversationally or more theatrically, depending on the context and your client's willingness to engage with a more energetic approach. It could take the form of a simple coaching question, such as 'Think of someone you admire and respect for their ability as a leader. Imagine standing in their shoes for a moment. What would you be thinking, feeling and experiencing?'

'As if' techniques are good for building confidence, practising different thoughts or behaviours and realizing that we all have a wider repertoire of behaviours than we routinely use. 'As if' techniques can also help with goal-setting, action planning and envisioning different futures.

Associating current behaviours with long-term consequences

I remember seeing a morbidly obese, housebound woman being interviewed on a television programme. She was asked by the reporter, 'How did you get this way?' She replied wistfully, 'very slowly'. It pained me to hear her response. Unless we stop and assess where our current choices and behaviours are going to take us, we can find ourselves in a place we did not want to be. Therefore, another key coaching approach is to encourage clients to associate their everyday behaviours and choices with long-term outcomes. The result of this can be either confirmation for the client that they are on the right path, or a moment of truth when they realize what the long-term outcome could be if they do not make some changes. This can be done conversationally: 'If you keep doing the same thing for the next so many years, what will that be like for you and what will have changed? How will you feel then, if everything is the same as it is now?' Alternatively, you can use movement, metaphor, acting 'as if' and changing perspective. An example of this would be to invite your client to imagine being a future version of themselves, after making no changes.

Associating everyday behaviours with long-term outcomes is useful for clients who are unhappy with their current situation but are lacking the motivation to change. It can also help if someone is considering a life or career change and is at a crossroads, uncertain which direction to take.

Zones of Exploration

Rather than thinking in terms of specific models or techniques, you can also think about your coaching approach in terms of zones of exploration. Most clients are looking for change in some way or another and change can be hard, even change we say we want to make. To be thorough in your quest to support your client, make sure that you explore all the following zones throughout a coaching assignment. You do not need to cover these in any particular order or refer to them explicitly in talking to the client. But use them as a mental checklist. It is certainly not exhaustive; you should feel free to add more zones of exploration yourself.

Beginnings zone

Explore the beginning or origin of the situation your client is in. Sample coaching questions:
- What triggered this?
- When was the first time you became aware of this?
- What else was happening around that time?
- What has changed since then?
- What have you done to date to make changes?

Assumptions zone

Explore both positive and negative beliefs and assumptions about the client's situation. Sample coaching questions:

- What beliefs or assumptions do you have about yourself, others or the world in general which underpin this situation?
- Which of those beliefs and assumptions are useful to you?
- Which of those beliefs and assumptions are hindering you?
- Whose voice do you hear when you think about this?
- What would be a more useful, or realistic set of beliefs you could have about this?

Impact zone

Explore what is the real impact on the client's life. Sample coaching questions:

- What does this behaviour or situation cost you?
- What benefit does this behaviour or situation give you?
- How would you be without this behaviour or situation?
- What is the impact on the wider system you are in, e.g. family, team or organization?

- What is one good reason to keep things as they are?
- What is one good reason to change?
- How much does this matter to you?

Familiarity zone

Explore what the client is doing to perpetuate the situation. Sample coaching questions:

- What things do you say and do that perpetuate this behaviour/situation?
- When do you experience exceptions to the usual behaviour/situation?
- What can you learn from the exceptions?
- How long have you been doing this?
- What different things could you say and do that would bring about a change?
- Which underused aspects of yourself could you bring into play?

Obstacles and strengths zone

Explore what is blocking your client and what strengths could assist them. Sample coaching questions:

- What internal and external obstacles are preventing you from addressing this change?
- What competing priorities or needs do you have that are taking priority?
- What matters most to you about this?
- What are you like when you are at your best?
- When have you succeeded before in your life?
- What are you bringing with you to this situation in terms of experience, wisdom, support, knowledge, confidence?

New behaviours zone

Explore how your client can experiment with some new behaviours. Sample coaching questions:

- How, when and with whom could you safely practise making a change?
- How far are you prepared to practise some different behaviours in the coaching room?
- What is the ultimate challenging situation in which you could try out your new behaviours?
- What would someone else, whom you admire and respect, do or say in this situation?

Maintenance zone

Explore how your client will keep going, working towards their goals and maintaining the changes they are making. Sample coaching questions:

- How will you remember to keep doing this?
- What could derail you from your plan?
- What strategy do you have in case you relapse?
- Who can support you to keep going?
- What or whom do you need to avoid?

Evidence zone (to be explored when changes are in place)

Explore and collect evidence of change. Sample coaching questions:

- What has changed?
- How do you know?
- What feedback, if any, have you had from other people?
- What are the benefits of the change?

In summary, you can approach the use of coaching tools in many ways. You can, like Melissa in Case Study 10.1, develop a structured programme around a few coaching techniques. You can keep a hard copy of coaching tools with you when you are coaching and pick out the appropriate tool at the appropriate moment. In time and with practice, you will probably be able to do this without the hard copies. You can approach your coaching in terms of zones of exploration, employing different techniques in any of the zones. You can rely heavily on listening and questioning, using tools and concepts conversationally.

Whichever techniques you favour, of the many hundreds of others that are available to coaches, it is essential to understand the principles that underpin them. This will give you more flexibility in how you choose to employ the models. You should also be aware of the pitfalls of only working with your preferred tools, and remember the benefits of constantly trying new ones.

Reflection Exercise for Coaches

What type of coach are you?

How would you describe your style of coaching? For example, are you challenging, supportive, creative, process-driven? How close is your coaching approach to mentoring, consultancy, training or counselling? Do you incorporate a wide range of techniques and flex your approach to your clients' needs or do you stick to the approaches you favour?

- What approaches do you shy away from and what is the reason for this?
- What approaches do you favour and why?
- What or who has informed your coaching approach?
- Reflect on what might be the benefits and the downsides, to both you and your coaching clients, of your coaching approach
- What, if anything, would you like to change about the type of coach you are?

Suggested Further Reading

Lasher, C. (2015) *Better Thinking for Better Results*. St Albans: Panoma Press Ltd.

Megginson, D. and Whitaker, V. (2007) *Continuing Professional Development,* 2nd edn. London: Kogan Page Limited.

Schein, E. and Van Maanen, J. (2013) *Career Anchors: The Changing Nature of Careers: Self-Assessment*. San Francisco, CA: Wiley.

Watts, R.E., Peluso, P.R. and Lewis, T.F. (2005) Expanding the acting as if technique: An Adlerian/constructive integration, *Journal of Individual Psychology*, 61(4): 380–7.

11 Self-Care for Coaches

This chapter looks at all the ways in which you can practise self-care. Self-care can be physical, emotional, spiritual, social, psychological, financial and professional, and each of us will have our own specific blend of elements which will nourish and restore us. Practising self-care as a coach is not selfish. In fact, clients learn more from what coaches do than from what coaches say, and it is important to role-model the behaviours that your clients aspire to. If your clients see you exhibiting compassion towards yourself, they will experience you as congruent and authentic in encouraging them to treat themselves with kindness and will be more likely to follow your lead (see Case Study 11.1).

Avoiding Exhaustion and Compassion Fatigue

Like many other professionals who help people, coaches are not always great at taking care of themselves. As the Buddhist and author Jack Kornfield (1994: 28) says, 'If your compassion does not include yourself, it is incomplete.' It is easy to neglect ourselves, particularly if we love the work we do as coaches and find it more fulfilling and less stressful than our previous roles. Some coaches even say that it does not feel like work. It can be all too easy to keep giving to others because we love what we do, because we enjoy making a difference to people's lives and we get a sense of meaning and purpose from it for ourselves. However, there are very many good reasons why it is vitally important for coaches to get into the habit of practising self-care from the beginning of their coaching careers.

Even if you get a buzz from coaching, it is still an emotionally and psychologically demanding process. You can be left at the end of a session with a bewildering range of feelings. You may have absorbed these from the client or they may be feelings of your own, experienced in response to the client. Sometimes a strong desire to help others can result in a feeling of disappointment that you did not help the client enough. All these emotional responses are valuable information and you will need time to process them away from the coaching session. Paying attention to your own thoughts and feelings is essential to prevent you from experiencing burnout, exhaustion or compassion fatigue or just from becoming careless in your practice.

Taking time to think about your own needs and responses will enable you to give your clients the best possible experience. If you have become a coach and a self-employed business person at the same time, you can find yourself with two compelling reasons to keep working: the first is that you love your new-found coaching career and enjoy seeing other people flourish. The second is that you now have no other means of sustaining yourself financially and you feel compelled to prioritize getting paid work above all other needs. You may find yourself saying 'yes' to every coaching opportunity and end up feeling overwhelmed.

I have heard it said that being self-employed can mean that you have the worst boss you have ever had in your life. Which other boss would treat you the way you treat yourself, expecting you to work long hours, evenings and weekends included, with no overtime, no holidays and no praise or recognition either?

You need to make a conscious decision to stop and reflect on how to practise care and compassion towards yourself, if you have been experiencing any of the following:

- Stress or anxiety
- Work–life balance out of kilter
- Having no interests outside of your work
- Loss of interest in coaching
- Feeling stale or uninspired about your work
- Doubting your ability as a coach
- Feeling resentful of the time and energy you give to your work
- Feeling resentful of your clients
- Not taking holidays
- Not exercising
- Excessive dependence on technology or using technology when you are meant to be resting or going to bed
- Taking on more work than you can competently handle
- Becoming fixated on winning the next contract
- Working long hours without proper breaks
- Neglecting your health, appearance, social life and other relationships in favour of work
- Not taking time to reflect on your thoughts and feelings
- Experiencing health-related issues

Walking your Talk

Case Study 11.1: Sushma

Before becoming a coach, Sushma had a really demanding job in financial services. She worked long hours and didn't take holidays; although she earned a lot of money, it was no compensation for her stressful lifestyle and its impact on her well-being. Eventually her marriage broke down and so did Sushma. She left her job and re-evaluated her life. Sushma booked herself onto all kinds of personal development workshops and retreats. She took up yoga and mindfulness and engaged a coach to help her change her life.

When Sushma decided to become a coach, she determined to take the lessons from her past into her future working life. Sushma set specific goals for her business, which included how many days she would work each year, how many days she would take as holiday and how many days she would invest in her personal and professional development. Sushma has a business coach, a supervisor, a personal trainer and spends six weeks every year on a retreat. Her approach to being a business owner is inspirational to her clients, most of whom are overworked entrepreneurs and business leaders. She shares her story with her clients and is proud to demonstrate how coaching helped her live a balanced life. Sushma often wonders why clients work with coaches who advocate work–life balance and self-care but don't do it for themselves. She knows that she would not engage a coach who didn't walk their talk.

Recognizing signs of burnout

If you had high-achieving, perfectionist tendencies before you became a coach, it is likely that you will have brought those tendencies with you into your coaching practice. Because you are passionate about what you do, you may find yourself working long hours, taking on too much work and putting pressure on yourself to over-deliver and excel in your work. You may not even notice how much pressure you are putting on yourself.

Even when you are working for yourself and loving what you do, working like this can lead to burnout if you do not make a conscious decision to practise self-care. Signs of burnout include loss of motivation, enthusiasm and creativity, feeling emotionally numb and having a generally negative outlook. Other signs are physical and mental exhaustion and questioning the value of what you are doing. Working 12-hour days and taking on lots of work can be exciting and give you a sense of achievement and success. However, it is not a sustainable strategy for most people. You can get so addicted to the rush of working and to the acknowledgement which comes with it that you can lose touch with the value of taking time out to reflect and take stock. Some people even get to the point where they feel guilty and at a loss if they are not working.

Having time and space to reflect on your coaching practice and your business activities is essential to your own health and to the health of your business.

Case Study 11.2: Diana

Diana has been coaching for over three years. She worked as a PR consultant in a fast-paced agency in London for over 30 years before retraining as a coach. Diana's background in PR enabled her to promote and market her business quickly and successfully and she is now in high demand for her one-to-one executive coaching services. She is very proud of her success as a coach and a business woman and pushes herself to achieve higher and higher sales targets each year.

Diana has not had any further development since her initial coach training and has never received supervision. She says that she had all the training she needed on her coach training programme and does not feel the need to acquire more skills or qualifications.

Diana typically works 12-hour days. Her original plans for a better work–life balance have lapsed. She over-commits herself and gets a buzz from winning clients, but is finding it hard to create the time and energy to give her clients the level of service she promises. She sees several clients each day and has no time to reflect between sessions. Sometimes she struggles to recall what happened in her clients' previous sessions because they are all beginning to become a blur.

When she first started coaching, Diana felt energized by the process. However, she has recently been feeling a bit stale and uninspired about the coaching she is doing. She has fallen into a formulaic way of working with her clients and is starting to lose enthusiasm.

She thinks she might be suffering from 'compassion fatigue', particularly when she works with highly privileged people who complain and are not happy with their lives. She is wondering now whether coaching was the right career choice for her after all.

How do you Practise Self-Care and Keep Energized if you are a Coach?

Here are some suggestions and ideas of ways in which you can take care of yourself. Ensure that you develop a self-care plan that includes some of the following.

Continuous professional development

When you are self-employed, you are responsible for your own development. You do not have an employer providing talent programmes, development opportunities or training courses for you. You do not have bosses or colleagues who could provide valuable learning as informal mentors. When you are a self-employed coach you have to create these development opportunities for yourself. Coaching is a fast-moving industry and new areas of research and interest appear all the time. It is important to keep informed about current trends and discussions and to develop opinions about them.

As a self-employed coach you have a responsibility to commit to maintaining and deepening your coaching knowledge and to developing your personal skills and self-awareness in ways which will benefit you, your practice and your clients. Above all, coaches are practitioners and therefore a lot of learning about coaching happens on the job. Coaches learn so much from being with other coaches. I often notice how coaches collect great coaching questions from one another and enjoy sharing knowledge, resources and best practice. Continuous professional development (CPD) for coaches can take many different forms beyond attending workshops and conferences and reading coaching books and publications. It can also mean attending coaching networking groups, peer coaching sessions and mastermind groups, accessing online learning summits and webinars and watching TED talks and YouTube videos.

The professional coaching bodies, such as the International Coach Federation (ICF), the European Mentoring & Coaching Council (EMCC) and the Association for Coaching (AC), all exist to maintain standards of competence and good practice and all provide easily accessible CPD for their members. All professional bodies that provide accreditation for coaches require evidence of CPD attended when you renew your coaching credentials with them.

Organizations that buy in coaching services also increasingly ask questions of external coaches about their credentials, supervisors and commitment to CPD. Committing to CPD is an indicator of your professional commitment to excellence.

Time to review your mission and purpose

If you are feeling stale or uninspired by your work, like Diana in Case Study 11.2, it is probably time to review your mission and purpose and get back in touch with the reasons you became a coach in the first place. Think back to what drew you to the work and how you imagined it would be. Recall what your hopes and dreams were for your coaching business and for you within that business. What did you think a typical working week would look like for you and how did you expect to feel about it? What did you do this for? What was it going to give you that you did not already have?

Now compare your expectations with the reality. What is different between the two and what is similar? What has interfered with your working life being the way you wanted it to be? How much have you personally influenced this? What, if any, repeating patterns do you notice from your life before you were a coach? Do you still have the same dreams as you had before? If so, what needs to change for you to have the life and the work you aspire to? What do you need to stop doing and what do you need to start doing? Who can offer you support? If your original mission has changed, then rework it and restate it to yourself. What do you need to do to make this happen for you? What is the most important thing you need to do each day to create the business and the life you want? How can you make sure that you do it?

Voluntary work

Doing some voluntary coaching or other work can be part of your self-care plan too. Volunteering your services will help you to make a real difference to individuals or organizations that could not otherwise afford them. Giving for the sake of giving can give you a sense of pride, satisfaction and purpose and you will probably learn some new skills and meet new people along the way: 'Not everything that counts can be counted. And not everything that can be counted counts' (Cameron 1963: 13).

I have met some coaches who become so focused on generating income that they lose sight of all the other reasons they were drawn to coaching in the first place and also lose sight of the rest of their lives. Many such coaches tell themselves, 'I am nearly there. If I keep working harder and earning more money, I will be securing a financial future for myself and then I will stop and do all the things I want to do.' When I have talked to coaches who have found themselves in this position, they have said that they lose sight of where 'there' is and that they keep moving the targets so that, when they eventually stop, it may be too late for them to do all those things they wanted to do. If you are feeling stressed, overwhelmed and overcommitted, then doing some voluntary work can give you a new sense of perspective and a reality check about the wider world.

Get a coach

Having a coach is another effective way of learning about coaching. Experiencing coaching as a client gives you a firmer grasp of the experience and value of being coached. You will learn from your own perspective what makes the coaching more effective or less effective and you will have an awareness of this learning when, in turn, you are coaching your clients. If a coach says to me, 'I don't really think I did anything in my coaching session. I don't know if I gave my client value', I question whether they have a coach themselves. When you are coached, you get a better sense of the value you are giving your clients. There is no doubt that when you are a coaching client, you unconsciously absorb some of the approaches your coach uses with you. If you are a coach who is also being coached, learning from your own coach will feed into the sessions you have with your own clients. Think what message you are giving about the value you place on coaching if your client asks you 'Do you have a coach?' and your answer is 'no'.

Don't rely on a single source of self-esteem

You will often see coaching clients who derive all their self-esteem from their status at work, or their role as a parent, or their physical prowess, and when something happens to weaken that source of self-esteem, they experience a loss of confidence or an identity crisis. As a coach, you take the same risk if you depend entirely on your professional life to give you a sense of self-worth. Coaching can be a very compelling and all-consuming occupation. It can also be such a passion for you that the lines between work and personal life can be blurred.

The solution is to explore areas of interest unrelated to coaching. Take up a hobby, read fiction (not just coaching or management books), spend time with friends and family and explore activities that are nothing to do with your coaching work. Revisit for yourself that old coaching favourite, the Wheel of Life, to see what your life balance looks like and how you can adjust it.

Giving time to activities unrelated to coaching will not only refresh you and enrich your life, it will also improve your coaching and enable you to model for your clients a healthier approach to work.

Keep a journal

Keeping a journal can increase your self-awareness and promote psychological and emotional growth. Committing to keeping a journal means that you are engaging in regular self-reflection.

Journaling allows you to reflect on your feelings, thoughts and behaviours throughout your life. It gives you the opportunity to examine your interactions with other people and to look at situations or relationships from new perspectives. There are no real rules about journaling, although it works best if you write regularly, without waiting for something special to write about. You can write in a free-flow, stream of consciousness way or you can decide to reflect on a specific coaching session, a coaching client or an aspect of yourself or your life. Since your journal entries are just for you, they can be scribbled or full of spelling mistakes or doodles. They can be painful, cathartic self-disclosures or practical to-do lists. They can make you laugh or cry. They can help you make plans or lead you to ponder and wonder about your life.

In your journal you can write inspirational quotes, song lyrics or poems that you love. You can capture your dreams when you wake up in the morning or your thoughts when you go to bed at night. You can write three good things that have happened each day or something you are grateful for. You can write about your mistakes and your fears, alongside your successes, hopes and dreams. You can write down things your clients have said about you and the work you are doing with them.

Our days are often crammed with moments and events. We may think we will remember the important words we have heard and the feelings we have experienced, but we probably will not unless we write them down. The real value in journaling is in stepping back and evaluating our thoughts, feelings and experiences. We need to read our journals regularly and become curious about how we represent our experiences in our writing. Reflecting on the reflective writing deepens our learning about ourselves.

Look after your physical well-being

As a coach, you are likely to spend a lot of your time sitting down, and too often hunched over a piece of technology. Coaching is a sedentary profession. When you are not sitting with a client or in front of your laptop or in a meeting, you may be in a car, a train or a plane. A coaching relationship is led by the client's agenda and I have seen this taken to extremes by some coaches. For example, I know coaches who ignore their own bladders and sit in discomfort, smiling and listening to their clients, fearful of interrupting the conversation and yet bursting to go to the loo. I recently spoke to a medical professional about this very phenomenon who told me it is a common problem for nurses, who are so used to responding to their patients that they ignore their own physical needs and cause themselves discomfort and even damage.

As this is not a book about exercise and well-being, I am not going to tell you what to do to keep fit and healthy – I am sure you already know what you should be doing. However, here are some coaching questions for you to reflect on:

- Which aspects of your physical health need attention?
- What is stopping you from prioritizing your own well-being?
- What one change would make the biggest difference to your health and well-being?
- How are your current behaviours benefiting you?
- What are your current behaviours costing you?
- Imagine meeting yourself in five years' time and discovering that you have not changed your behaviours regarding exercise, fresh air, health, well-being. How do you experience that future version of yourself?

Identify repeating patterns in your life and work

Case Study 11.3: Sam

Sam has spent her working life in the caring professions: first as a nurse, followed by a career in the voluntary sector and finally retraining as a coach. Sam offers coaching to women who are not in paid work and who have few educational or vocational qualifications. She specializes in building her clients' confidence and working with them on career planning.

Sam's clients love her and she has many success stories. In fact, many of her clients keep in touch and keep her updated on their progress. The pinboard in her office is covered in 'thank you' cards and letters. In fact, she builds such good relationships with her clients that they never lose touch with her and she spends a good deal of time replying to emails and phone calls from past clients. This is not paid work, it's just Sam being nice.

> Sam feels permanently exhausted and works for at least 12 hours every day. She has recently been suffering from stress and exhaustion. She is starting to feel resentment towards some her clients for demanding so much from her and is envious of other coaches who achieve a work–life balance and earn more money than she does. She does not have a meaningful social life or hobbies or activities outside of her work.

If, like Sam in Case Study 11.3, you have always been a caring person with a desire to make things better for others, it is likely that you will bring all those same tendencies into your work as a coach. Stephen Karpman (1968) developed a psychological model of human interaction associated with transactional analysis. His model is known as the Karpman Drama Triangle.

The model presents three roles that are often adopted in relationships: the victim, the persecutor and the rescuer. Put simply, a persecutor will blame or bully a victim, who has feelings of inadequacy and helplessness, and the rescuer will swoop in to make things better. Karpman, who as well as being a student of Eric Berne, the father of transactional analysis, was a member of the Screen Actors' Guild, was interested in the dynamic process by which people are drawn into the game and then swap roles, rotating around the triangle. At the same time, he recognized that people are inclined to play one role more than the others. His model invites us to explore what benefit we receive, consciously or unconsciously, from the roles we habitually play. Could it be that the victim does not really want to be rescued or that the rescuer does not want the victim to stop needing them? There is a danger that, without adequate supervision, people in helping professions can become dependent on their rescuer tendencies. Feeling needed gives the rescuer a sense of self-worth and power. Focusing on rescuing someone else also allows the rescuer to avoid looking at themselves because the victim's needs are more pressing.

Sam's case study suggests that pleasing others at the expense of pleasing yourself can lead to pent-up feelings of resentment towards those we appear to be helping willingly. Sam is being dishonest towards her clients in inviting them to stay in touch with her, with apparent generosity, while silently resenting them for taking advantage of her time and good nature. Such people-pleasing behaviours can be the result of conditioning in early life. For example, children who struggle to attain the love or attention of their parents or who have to take on responsibility for the family too young often grow up with a heightened desire to please others. You may have developed a belief early in life that people will reject you or leave you if you are not nice to them and this message can become deeply ingrained and magnified in adult life. You may believe that being overly nice to others will protect you from rejection. Or you may believe that as a reward for doing people favours or giving them compliments, you will get something nice back from them, which will boost your self-esteem.

The biggest problem with excessive people-pleasing or rescuing is that you are compromising your integrity. You are not acting in line with how you are really thinking and feeling, which leaves you resentful and unfulfilled. If you are a coach with excessive rescuer or people-pleaser tendencies, you need to establish and maintain clear boundaries with your clients. In Sam's case, this would mean, for example, renegotiating a contract with her past clients to give them the option of paying an annual fee for a certain number of follow-up calls or emails.

Work with a coaching supervisor

Attending regular supervision sessions is an essential aspect of your self-care. Working with a supervisor will give you the time and space to explore some of the patterns and behaviours that derail you from peak performance as a coach. The repeating patterns of your relationships with others is an important topic to explore in supervision sessions or as part of your reflective practice. Unless you address the underlying motivations that are driving your behaviour, the behaviour will invariably continue to show up in your relationships with clients. There are two people in every coaching session: the coach and the client. The coach's role requires an ongoing commitment to enhancing their own self-awareness. High levels of self-awareness enable coaches to notice what is going on for them in a coaching session, and to acknowledge what is separate and different from what is going on for their clients. Supervision continues to raise self-awareness for coaches and enables them to own their part in any challenges or difficulties in their coaching relationships.

So, what stops coaches accessing supervision? Some coaches think that they will start having supervision when they get some clients, or when they have some really juicy case studies to present to their supervision or supervision group. Remember that you don't need to have clients to attend supervision. If you don't have any clients, you may avoid supervision because it represents yet another financial outlay when you are not earning any money from coaching. Spending time thinking about your coaching in the presence of other coaches can give you ideas, support, challenge and motivation. A supervision group may well normalize your current situation – you may find you are not the only coach who is struggling to find paying clients. You will be able to consider what could be getting in the way of you finding clients and what actions you could take to secure your first client. Supervision can keep you going through a challenging time at the start of your business. Supervision provides continued learning and development for you after your coach training programme has finished.

More experienced coaches might think they are too busy, can't spare the time or think that they are doing fine and don't need supervision. Supervision can bring to the surface blind spots and challenge complacency if you have got to the point of thinking you don't need to reflect on your practice.

Sometimes coaches feel that, unless they have a glaringly obvious problem, they do not require supervision. You will find that development often comes merely from the process of sharing your coaching experiences and reflecting on them. In addition, the supervisor will pick up on patterns, limiting beliefs and areas for development, providing clarity and an objective view.

Supervision can be delivered one-to-one or in a group with a number of other coaches. The purpose is to gain perspective and a measure of objectivity on your own coaching work, particularly in complex or difficult situations or in work that triggers emotional responses in you. It is also an opportunity to gain reassurance when you are doubting yourself, and support in the form of information and ideas.

In the field of counselling and psychotherapy, Francesca Inskipp and Brigid Proctor (1995) have identified three key functions of supervision: 'normative, formative and restorative'. These headings are equally applicable to coaching supervision.

The normative role of the supervisor involves ensuring that the coach is complying with accepted professional standards and operating within the appropriate codes of ethics. Supervision is formative in the sense that the process encourages the coach to develop the skills and acquire the knowledge necessary to become an increasingly effective practitioner. At an emotional level, the supervisor provides a restorative function by listening, supporting and championing the coach through doubts and insecurities, while challenging and inspiring them to be better.

The process usually involves the coach reporting on a current case to the supervisor. The supervisor encourages the coach to reflect on the issues the case raises in order to achieve a deeper understanding of what is happening for their client and for themselves, and to consider how to proceed. Supervision enhances the competence and self-awareness of the coach. This level of support, development and containment means that there is a greater chance of the needs of the coaching client being met by the coach.

When I started working with my current coaching supervisor, I asked what her fees were. She told me she charges the same hourly fee which I charge to my clients. This made me immediately uncomfortable because I couldn't say what my hourly fee was. I operated a very wide sliding scale, which depended on the client, their role, how much I wanted to help them and as far as I could tell, what day of the week it was. There was no clear process. I went away and averaged out my hourly fee. It was shockingly low. I was then worried to tell my supervisor. Would she think I had fabricated a low fee so that I didn't have to pay her as much? I doubted she would think this, but if she believed me, I felt embarrassed to tell her that I wasn't charging anywhere close to my going rate. This revelation and subsequent discussion formed the basis of our first few supervision sessions. My supervisor recognized my inability to acknowledge my worth and challenged me to develop stronger boundaries about fees. My predisposition for self-sacrifice has surfaced time and again in supervision in relation to other client dilemmas and even in my position as a business leader. My supervisor skilfully weaves together themes from all areas of my life to enhance my understanding of my part in the ethical and contractual dilemmas in my coaching practice.

Coaching Exercises

What does your client learn from you?

Imagine being one of your clients. Experience what it is like to be on the receiving end of your questions, the way you build rapport, how you support and challenge and how you maintain boundaries.

As one of your clients, think about what other messages you pick up from you. Think about how you speak about yourself, how you demonstrate care for yourself, your health, your time and your value. Notice any incongruence between the ideas and attitudes you promote as a coach and the way you live your life.

- Still seeing through the eyes of one of your clients, make a note of all the qualities and behaviours exhibited by your coach that you would like to emulate.
- Now make a note of all the qualities and behaviours of your coach that you would not want to emulate.
- Now, returning to your own shoes, consider what changes you could make that would increase your integrity and consistency.

Letter to your boss

This is an exercise for self-employed coaches.

Write a letter to your boss (yes, that's you) telling them all the great things they do for you and all the things they could do better.

- Think about support and learning opportunities, your working hours and working conditions, your hourly rate of pay, how many days' holidays you get each year, whether your boss honours the fact that you are on holiday, the responsibilities you are expected to fulfil and the expectations placed on you.
- What would you like to be different so that you could say that you had a fair, supportive and inspiring boss?
- What can you do to make this happen?

Self-care plan

Your business plan should include a self-care plan. Based on all the ideas in this chapter, and any others of your own, put together a realistic plan to nourish, develop and sustain yourself in your coaching work.

How will you care for yourself: physically, emotionally, psychologically, socially, spiritually, financially, professionally and educationally?

Design some self-care strategies for each of the above categories. Decide how often you are going to do them and what you will do to ensure that you maintain momentum. From what or whom will you need support?

For each category, express clearly why you are adopting the strategy you have chosen. What will happen to you, your business or your clients if you do not do this? What will doing this give you that you would not otherwise have?

Suggested Further Reading

Brown, B. (2015) *Daring Greatly: How the Courage to Be Vulnerable Transforms the Way We Live, Love, Parent and Lead*. London: Penguin Group.

Hall, L. (2013) *Mindful Coaching: How Mindfulness Can Transform Coaching Practice*. London: Kogan Page Limited.

Narain, N. and Narain-Phillips, K. (2017) *Self-Care for the Real World: Practical Self-Care Advice for Everyday Life*. London: Hutchinson.

Conclusion and Closing Comments

Thank you for reading this book.

I want to thank all the many coaches I have trained, coached, mentored and supervised over the years. You have told me about your dreams, hopes and fears as you embark on your careers in coaching. You have shared your disappointments, milestones and triumphs as coaching professionals and business owners. What I have learned from you has inspired me to write this book.

I have admiration for all of you who are continually working to be the best coaches you can be. I recognize the courage it takes to embrace personal and professional change. It takes a special sort of person to undertake a demanding course of study, to change career, perhaps to start a business, to coach. You all have in common a commitment to enabling others to lead more fulfilled, happier and more fruitful lives.

I hope this book has provided you with some useful information, resources and support in your continuing development as a coach.

I have a strong belief in the power of normalization and its role in building confidence. Therefore, I hope that the examples and case studies in the book have given you a sense that you are not alone and that most coaches, at some time or another, struggle with similar challenges and dilemmas . . . and it is in these moments of puzzlement that more learning and growth occurs.

I wish you plenty of moments to sit back, acknowledge and celebrate how far you have come. I wish you more states of puzzlement, more learning, and every success in the work you do.

References

CHAPTER 1 – Credibility

Coleman, H.J. (1996) *Empowering Yourself: The Organizational Game Revealed.* Dubuque, IA: Kendall/Hunt.

International Coach Federation (ICF), PricewaterhouseCoopers LLP (2016) *Global Coaching Survey.* Lexington, KY: International Coach Federation.

Mann C. (2016) *6th Ridler Report.* London: Ridler & Co.

Suzuki, S. (1970) *Zen Mind, Beginners Mind.* New York: Walker/Weatherhill.

CHAPTER 2 – Building a Coaching Business

Department for Business, Innovation and Skills (2010), *BIS Small Business Survey.* Sheffield: BIS. Available at https://www.gov.uk/government/publications/small-business-survey-2010 [Accessed January 2019].

Forbes, B.C. (1915) *Finance, Business and the Business of Life.* New York: The author.

International Coach Federation (ICF), PricewaterhouseCoopers LLP (2016) *Global Coaching Survey.* Lexington, KY: International Coach Federation.

Small Business Trends (2010) *A Business Plan Doubles Your Chances for Success, Says a New Survey.* Available at https://smallbiztrends.com/2010/06/business-plan-success-twice-as-likely.html [Accessed January 2019].

StartUp Britain (2016). *Startup Tracker.* Available at: http://www.startupbritain.org/startup-tracker [Accessed 17 August 2018].

CHAPTER 3 – Overcoming Impostor Syndrome

Burch, N. (1970s) *The Conscious Competence Framework.* Solana Beach, CA: Gordon Training International.

Casement, P. (1985) *On Learning from the Patient.* London and New York: Tavistock Publications.

Clance, P.R. (1985) *The Impostor Phenomenon: Overcoming the Fear that Haunts Your Success.* Atlanta, GA: Peachtree Publishers.

Clance, P.R. and Imes, S.A. (1978) The Imposter Phenomenon in high achieving women: dynamics and therapeutic intervention, *Psychotherapy Theory, Research and Practice*, 15(3): 241–7.

Gallwey, W.T. (1974) *The Inner Game of Tennis.* New York: Random House.

International Coach Federation (ICF), PricewaterhouseCoopers LLP (2016) *Global Coaching Survey.* Lexington, KY: International Coach Federation.

Kruger, J. and Dunning, D. (1999) Unskilled and unaware of it: How difficulties in recognizing one's own incompetence lead to inflated self-assessments, *Journal of Personality and Social Psychology*, 77(6): 1121–34.

Mezirow, J.D. (1991) *Transformative Dimensions of Adult Learning*. San Francisco, CA: Jossey-Bass.

Perls, F.S., Hefferline, R.F. and Goodman, P. (1951) *Gestalt Therapy: Excitement and Growth in the Human Personality*. New York: Bantam Books.

Sherpa Coaching LLC (2017) *12th Annual Industry Review*. Cincinnati, OH: Sasha Corporation.

CHAPTER 4 – Contracting, Pitching and Client Meetings

Mann, C. (2016) *6th Ridler Report*. London: Ridler & Co.

CHAPTER 5 – Managing Client Boundaries

International Coach Federation (ICF) (2015) *Code of Ethics*. Available at https://coachfederation.org/code-of-ethics [Accessed 17 August 2018].

CHAPTER 6 – Boundaries of Time and Place

Kline, N. (1999) *Time to Think: Listening to Ignite the Human Mind*. London: Cassell Illustrated.

CHAPTER 7 – Facilitating Change

De Haan, E. (2008) *Relational Coaching: Journeys Towards Mastering One-to-One Learning*. Chichester: John Wiley & Sons Ltd.

Jarvis, P. (1995) Teachers and learners in adult education: Transaction or moral interaction?, *Studies in the Education of Adults*, 27(1): 24–35.

Mezirow, J.D. (1991) *Transformative Dimensions of Adult Learning*. San Francisco, CA: Jossey-Bass.

Neill, M. (2006) *You Can Have What You Want*. Carlsbad, CA: Hay House Inc.

Prochaska, J.O. and DiClemente, C.C. (1982) Transtheoretical therapy: Toward a more integrative model of change, *Psychotherapy: Theory, Research & Practice*, 19(3): 276–88.

Steinem, G. (1970) 'Women's liberation' aims to free men, too, *The Washington Post*, Sunday 7 June 1970.

CHAPTER 8 – Group Coaching

International Coach Federation (ICF), PricewaterhouseCoopers LLP (2016) *Global Coaching Survey*. Lexington, KY: International Coach Federation.

CHAPTER 10 – When Will I Know Enough?

Corey, G. (1996) *Theory and Practice of Counselling and Psychotherapy*, 5th edn. Pacific Grove, CA: Brooks/Cole.

De Haan, E., Culpin, V. and Curd, J. (2011) Executive coaching in practice: What determines helpfulness for clients of coaching?, *Personnel Review*, 40(1): 24–44.

Jung, C.G. (1933) *Modern Man in Search of a Soul*. Oxford: Harcourt, Brace.

Jung, C.G. (1953) *Psychological Reflections*. New York: Pantheon Books.

Rogers, C. (1951) *Client-Centered Therapy: Its Current Practice, Implications and Theory*. London: Constable.

CHAPTER 11 – Self-Care for Coaches

Cameron, W.J. (1963) *Informal Sociology: A Casual Introduction to Sociological Thinking*. New York: Random House.

Inskipp, F. and Proctor, B. (1995) *The Art, Craft and Tasks of Counselling Supervision. Part 2: Becoming a Supervisor*, 2nd edn. Twickenham: Cascade.

Karpman, S. (1968) Fairy tales and script drama analysis, *Transactional Analysis Bulletin*, 7(26): 39–43.

Kornfield, J. (1994) *Buddha's Little Instruction Book*. New York: Bantam Books.

Suggested Further Reading

CHAPTER 1 – Credibility

Coleman, H.J. (1996) *Empowering Yourself: The Organizational Game Revealed*. Dubuque, IA: Kendall/Hunt.

Duckworth, A. (2018) *Grit: The Power of Passion and Perseverance*. New York: Scribner.

Rogers, J. (2017) *Building a Coaching Business: Ten Steps to Success*, 2nd edn. London: Open University Press.

CHAPTER 2 – Building a Coaching Business

Brown, C. (2013) *Testing the Water: Helping You Take Your First Steps from Education to Work*. Tollerton, England: Barny Books.

Brown-Volkman, D. (2003) *Four Steps to Building a Profitable Coaching Practice: A Complete Marketing Resource Guide for Coaches*. Lincoln, NE: iUniverse Inc.

Gerber, M.E. (2001) *The E-Myth Revisited: Why Most Small Business Don't Work and What to Do About It*. New York: HarperCollins.

CHAPTER 3 – Overcoming Impostor Syndrome

Cuddy, A. (2016) *Presence: Bringing Your Boldest Self to Your Biggest Challenges*. London: Orion Publishing.

Goyder, C. (2014) *Gravitas: Communicate with Confidence, Influence and Authority*. London: Vermillion.

Watts, G. and Morgan, K. (2015) *The Coach's Casebook: Mastering the Twelve Traits That Trap Us*. Cheltenham: Inspect & Adapt Ltd.

CHAPTER 4 – Contracting, Pitching and Client Meetings

Chandler, S. and Litvin, R. (2013) *The Prosperous Coach: Increase Income and Impact for You and Your Clients*. Anna Maria, FL: Maurice Bassett.

Oade, A. (2008) *Starting and Running a Coaching Business: The Complete Guide to Setting Up and Managing a Coaching Practice*. Oxford: How To Books Ltd.

Rogers, J. (2016) *Coaching Skills: The Definitive Guide to Being a Coach*, 4th edn. Maidenhead: Open University Press.

CHAPTER 5 – Managing Client Boundaries

Egan, G. (2001) *The Skilled Helper: A Problem-Management Approach to Helping*, 4th edn. Pacific Grove, CA: Brooks/Cole Publishing Company.

Hay, J. (2007) *Reflective Practice and Supervision for Coaches*. Maidenhead: Open University Press.

Sandler, C. (2011) *Executive Coaching: A Psychodynamic Approach*. Maidenhead: Open University Press.

CHAPTER 6 – Boundaries of Time and Place

Casement, P. (1985) *On Learning from the Patient*. London and New York: Tavistock Publications.

Cloud, H. and Townsend, J. (2007) *Boundaries*. Grand Rapids, MI: Zondervan.

Passmore, J. (2011) *Supervision in Coaching: Supervision, Ethics and Continuous Professional Development*. London: Kogan Page Limited.

CHAPTER 7 – Facilitating Change

Dilts, R. (1990) *Changing Belief Systems with Neuro-Linguistic Programming*. Scotts Valley, CA: Dilts Strategy Group.

Kelly, R. and Allen, C. (2011) *Thrive*. Cambridge: Rob Kelly Publishing.

Prochaska, J.O. and Prochaska, J.M. (2016) *Changing to Thrive: Overcome the Top Risks to Lasting Health and Happiness*. Center City, MN: Hazelden Publishing.

CHAPTER 8 – Group Coaching

Britton, J.J. (2011) *Effective Group Coaching, Tried and Tested Tools and Resources for Optimum Coaching Results*. Mississauga, Canada: John Wiley & Sons Canada Ltd.

Rogers, J. (2007) *Adults Learning*, 5th edn. Maidenhead: Open University Press.

Thornton, T. (2010) *Group and Team Coaching (Essential Coaching Skills and Knowledge)*. Hove: Routledge.

CHAPTER 9 – Coaching Dilemmas

Ainsworth, E.R. (2016) *360 Degree Feedback: A Transformational Approach*. St Albans: Panama Press Ltd.

Hazler, R.J. and Barwick, N. (2001) *The Therapeutic Environment (Core Concepts in Therapy)*. Maidenhead: Open University Press.

O'Neill, M.B. (2000) *Executive Coaching with Backbone and Heart: A Systems Approach to Engaging Leaders with Their Challenges*. New York: Jossey-Bass.

CHAPTER 10 – When Will I Know Enough?

Lasher, C. (2015) *Better Thinking for Better Results*. St Albans: Panoma Press Ltd.

Megginson, D. and Whitaker, V. (2007) *Continuing Professional Development*, 2nd edn. London: Kogan Page Limited.

Schein, E. and Van Maanen, J. (2013) *Career Anchors: The Changing Nature of Careers: Self-Assessment*. San Francisco, CA: Wiley.

Watts, R.E., Peluso, P.R. and Lewis, T.F. (2005) Expanding the acting as if technique: An Adlerian/constructive integration, *Journal of Individual Psychology*, 61(4): 380–7.

CHAPTER 11 – Self-Care for Coaches

Brown, B. (2015) *Daring Greatly: How the Courage to Be Vulnerable Transforms the Way We Live, Love, Parent and Lead*. London: Penguin Group.

Hall, L. (2013) *Mindful Coaching: How Mindfulness Can Transform Coaching Practice*. London: Kogan Page Limited.

Narain, N. and Narain-Phillips, K. (2017) *Self-Care for the Real World: Practical Self-Care Advice for Everyday Life*. London: Hutchinson.

Index

360-degree feedback, coaching dilemmas 118–21

acting 'as if' technique, coaching tools and techniques 130–1
adult learning principles, group coaching 96
advertising and PR 10
  see also pitches/pitching
  profile raising 9–12
agreements, contracts/contracting 48
aims, this book's 1–2
anecdotes, pitches/pitching 51–2
appraisal, credibility 14–15
approaches, coaching *see* coaching approaches
areas of expertise, credibility 5
associating current behaviours with long-term consequences, coaching tools and techniques 131
association, credibility by 10–12
assumptions, credibility 5–6
assumptions zone, zones of exploration 132

background to the assignment, three-way meetings 45
beginnings and endings, time boundaries 74–5
beginnings zone, zones of exploration 132
boundary management
  see also client boundaries; meeting places
  coaching exercises 77–8
burnout, self-care for coaches 138–9
business, coaching 17–28
  charging for your services 20–3
  contracts/contracting 42–3
  marketing 18–20
  setting-up 17–18
  social media 18–20
  starting 17–18
  three-way meetings 43–7
business development
  coaching exercises 26–8
  ideal clients 27–8
  wheel of business focus 26
  wheel of entrepreneurial traits 26–7
business focus 26

business planning 23–5
  leadership and growth 25

cancellations, coaching dilemmas 111–13
change, facilitating *see* facilitating change
change vs transformation, facilitating change 79–80
changing perspective, coaching tools and techniques 130
changing places with clients, client boundaries 64
charging for your services 20–3
  price rise indicators 21–2
  pricing 19, 21–2
chemistry
  client boundaries 61–2
  coaching approaches 13
  credibility 12–14
client boundaries 54–64
  changing places with clients 64
  chemistry 61–2
  coaching exercises 64
  countertransference 62, 63
  crying clients 58
  first client 54–5
  friendship 59–60
  International Coach Federation's *Code of Ethics* 59
  off-duty as a coach 60–1
  reflective practice 64
  self-disclosure 55–8
client: organization or coachee? coaching dilemmas 113–16
clients, ideal, business development 27–8
clients' point of view, self-care for coaches 147
client's workplace, meeting places 69–70
coaching approaches 3
  chemistry 13
  facilitating change 80–2
  Impostor Syndrome 32–3, 36–7
  meeting places 72
  pitches/pitching 49–52
  self-disclosure 56
coaching business *see* business, coaching

coaching conundrums, coaching dilemmas
107–108
coaching dilemmas 107–123
360-degree feedback 118–21
cancellations 111–13
client: organization or coachee? 113–16
coaching conundrums 107–108
coaching exercises 122–3
coaching someone who is already working
with a coach or therapist 113
feedback 117–22
hidden agendas 115–16
no-shows 111–13
organizations 113–16
referrals 116–17
resistant clients 108–111, 113
role boundaries 117
self-reflection 122–3
unfinished coaching assignments 111–13
coaching exercises
boundary management 77–8
business development 26–8
client boundaries 64
coaching dilemmas 122–3
credibility 14–16
group coaching 105–106
Impostor Syndrome 40–1
limiting beliefs 91–3
pitches/pitching 53
self-care for coaches 147–8
coaching niche, Impostor Syndrome 39–40
coaching objectives, three-way meetings 45–6
coaching relationships 127–8
relationship coaching 8
'unconditional positive regard' 128
coaching someone who is already working with
a coach or therapist 113
coaching stance, group coaching 101–102
coaching tools and techniques 125–7
acting 'as if' technique 130–1
associating current behaviours with
long-term consequences 131
concepts and principles 129–31
conversational metaphors 129–30
diagrams 129–30
images 129–30
objects 129–30
perspective change 130
playing to preferences 126–7
reflection exercise for coaches 134–5
standard coaching processes 125–6
zones of exploration 132–5
co-coaches, working with 102–103
Code of Ethics, client boundaries 59

coffee shops, meeting places 72–3
compassion fatigue, self-care for coaches
136–7, 139
concepts and principles 129–31
confidence-building
group coaching 102
Impostor Syndrome 35, 36–8
limiting beliefs 87–93
confidentiality, three-way meetings 46
Conscious Competence Framework, Impostor
Syndrome 39
continuous professional development (CPD),
self-care for coaches 139–40
contracts/contracting 21, 22–3, 42–9
agreements 48
coaching business 42–3
formal contracting 48
group coaching 99
Impostor Syndrome 33–4
one-to-one clients 47–9
sample contracts 48–9
three-way meetings 43–7
conversational metaphors, coaching tools and
techniques 129–30
countertransference., client boundaries 62, 63
credibility 4–16
see also qualifications
appraisal 14–15
areas of expertise 5
by association 10–12
assumptions 5–6
chemistry 12–14
coaching exercises 14–16
environment changes 6–12
establishing 6–12
'fit' 5–6
increasing 14–16
networking 7, 8, 12, 16
new and different sectors 6–12
pro bono coaching experience 7
proving your credentials 4–6
by proxy 9
sphere of influence 16
subject matter experts 7–9
thought leaders 7–9

diagrams, coaching tools and techniques
129–30
dilemmas, coaching *see* coaching dilemmas
'door handle moments,' time boundaries 76
dream board members exercise,
pitches/pitching 53
Dunning-Kruger effect, Impostor Syndrome
36–7

entrepreneurial traits 26–7
environment changes, establishing credibility
    6–12
establishing credibility 6–12
ethics, International Coach Federation's *Code
    of Ethics* 59
evidence wall, Impostor Syndrome 40
evidence zone, zones of exploration 134
evidence-based practice, Impostor Syndrome 32
exercises, coaching *see* coaching exercises
exhaustion fatigue, self-care for coaches
    136–7
expectations about change, Impostor
    Syndrome 35–6
experience-building, Impostor Syndrome 36–8
exposure/performance/image 9–12

facilitating change 79–93
    action 84–5
    change models 81
    change vs transformation 79–80
    coaches' role 85–7
    coaching approaches 80–2
    commitment to change 83–4
    common elements 81–7
    critical moments 86–7
    desire to change 83–4
    experimentation 84–5
    gap between current reality and desired
        change 82–3
    how change happens 80–1
    limiting beliefs 87–93
    obstacles 82–3
    practice 84–5
    readiness to change 81–2
    transformational learning 87
    Transtheoretical Model of Change 84
    unlearning 84–5
false modesty, Impostor Syndrome 31
familiarity zone, zones of exploration 133
feedback
    coaching dilemmas 117–22
    three-way meetings 46
fees
    see also charging for your services
    supervision 146
'fit,' credibility 5–6
formal contracting, contracts/contracting 48
free association list, limiting beliefs 91–2
frequently asked questions 1
friendship, client boundaries 59–60

group coaching 94–106
    adult learning principles 96

celebration 101
coaching exercises 105–106
coaching stance 101–102
co-coaches, working with 102–103
confidence-building 102
contracts/contracting 99
groups 95
information and coaching resources 100
joy of 98–9
learning styles 100
in organizations 103–105
peer coaching 100
positive speaking 99–100
prerequisites 105–106
programme elements 99–101
reflection questions 105
session structures 98
skills 95–7
support-building 100–101
teams 95, 96–7
work between sessions 100
growth and leadership 25

having a coach, self-care for coaches 141
hidden agendas, coaching dilemmas
    115–16
home office, meeting places 68–9
honesty, pitches/pitching 52–3
hotel lobbies, meeting places 72–3

ideal clients, business development 27–8
image/exposure/performance 9–12
images, coaching tools and techniques
    129–30
impact zone, zones of exploration
    132–3
Impostor Syndrome 29–41
    coaching approaches 32–3, 36–7
    coaching exercises 40–1
    coaching niche 39–40
    confidence-building 35, 36–8
    Conscious Competence Framework 39
    contracts/contracting 33–4
    Dunning-Kruger effect 36–7
    evidence wall 40
    evidence-base practice 32
    expectations about change 35–6
    experience-building 36–8
    false modesty 31
    mentor coaching 37–8
    novice benefits 38–9
    'reading' clients 34–5
    reference, writing your own 40
    referrals 35

supervision 37–8
support-building 36–8
testimonials 35
training 30–3, 36–9
information and coaching resources, group
    coaching 100
intellectual property 21
International Coach Federation's *Code of
    Ethics*, client boundaries 59

jargon, pitches/pitching 51–2
journal, self-care for coaches 142

Karpman Drama Triangle, self-care for
    coaches 144

leadership and growth 25
learning styles, group coaching 100
letter to your boss, self-care for coaches 147
limiting beliefs 87–93
    coaching exercises 91–3
    free association list 91–2
    initial contracting conversations 89
    'Post-it' note exercise 92–3
    recognizing 90
    transformational learning 87–93
    working with 89–91

maintaining time boundaries 76–7
maintenance zone, zones of exploration 134
marketing
    coaching business 18–20
    social media 18–20
meeting places 66–74
    client's workplace 69–70
    coaching approaches 72
    coffee shops 72–3
    home office 68–9
    hotel lobbies 72–3
    online coaching 73–4
    outdoors 71
    private meeting rooms 70–1
    telephone coaching 73–4
    video-conferencing 73–4
meetings *see* three-way meetings
memorable pitches/pitching 52
mentor coaching, Impostor Syndrome 37–8
metaphors, conversational, coaching tools and
    techniques 129–30

networking, credibility 7, 8, 12, 16
new and different sectors, establishing
    credibility 6–12
new behaviours zone, zones of exploration 133

no-shows, coaching dilemmas 111–13
novice benefits, Impostor Syndrome 38–9

objectives, coaching 45–6
objects, coaching tools and techniques
    129–30
obstacles and strengths zone, zones of
    exploration 133
off-duty as a coach, client boundaries 60–1
one-to-one clients, contracts/contracting 47–9
online coaching 73–4
organizations
    client: organization or coachee? coaching
        dilemmas 113–16
    coaching dilemmas 113–16
    group coaching in 103–105
    resistant clients 108–111, 113
outdoors, meeting places 71

patterns, identifying repeating, self-care for
    coaches 143–5
peer coaching, group coaching 100
performance/image/exposure 9–12
person-centred approach, self-disclosure 56
perspective change, coaching tools and
    techniques 130
physical well-being, self-care for coaches 143
pitches/pitching 49–53
    see also advertising and PR; profile raising
    anecdotes 51–2
    coaching approaches 49–52
    coaching exercises 53
    dream board members exercise 53
    honesty 52–3
    jargon 51–2
    memorable 52
    preparation 50–1
    real-life examples 51–2
    selling yourself 53
places, meeting *see* meeting places
planning *see* business planning
playing to preferences, coaching tools and
    techniques 126–7
positive speaking, group coaching 99–100
'Post-it' note exercise, limiting beliefs 92–3
PR and advertising 10
    see also pitches/pitching
    profile raising 9–12
preparation, pitches/pitching 50–1
prerequisites, group coaching 105–106
presentations 49–53
    see also pitches/pitching
pricing *see* charging for your services
private meeting rooms, meeting places 70–1

pro bono coaching experience 7
profile raising 9–12
  see also pitches/pitching
programme elements, group coaching
    99–101
promoting your business *see* profile raising
proposals 49–53
  see also pitches/pitching
proving your credentials 4–6
proxy, credibility by 9

qualifications 4–5, 6, 124
  see also credibility

'reading' clients, Impostor Syndrome 34–5
real-life examples, pitches/pitching 51–2
reference, writing your own 40
referrals
  coaching dilemmas 116–17
  Impostor Syndrome 35
reflection, self-reflection 122–3
reflection exercise for coaches, coaching tools
    and techniques 134–5
reflection questions, group coaching 105
reflective practice, client boundaries 64
relationship coaching 8
resistant clients
  coaching dilemmas 108–111, 113
  organizations 108–111, 113
reviewing your mission and purpose, self-care
    for coaches 140–1
reviews, work 78
role boundaries, coaching dilemmas 117

sample contracts, contracts/contracting
    48–9
self-care for coaches 136–48
  burnout 138–9
  clients' point of view 147
  coaching exercises 147–8
  compassion fatigue 136–7, 139
  continuous professional development (CPD)
    139–40
  exhaustion fatigue 136–7
  having a coach 141
  journal, keeping a 142
  Karpman Drama Triangle 144
  letter to your boss 147
  patterns, identifying repeating 143–5
  physical well-being 143
  reviewing your mission and purpose
    140–1
  self-care plan 147–8
  self-esteem sources 141–2

supervision 145–6
  voluntary work 141
  walking your talk 137–9
  work-life balance 137–9
self-care plan, self-care for coaches 147–8
self-disclosure
  client boundaries 55–8
  coaching approaches 56
  person-centred approach 56
self-esteem sources, self-care for coaches
    141–2
self-reflection, coaching dilemmas 122–3
selling yourself *see* pitches/pitching
social media
  coaching business 18–20
  marketing 18–20
sphere of influence, credibility 16
'spreading the word' 10
standard coaching processes, coaching tools
    and techniques 125–6
subject matter experts, establishing credibility
    7–9
success measurement, three-way meetings 46
supervision
  fees 146
  functions 146
  Impostor Syndrome 37–8
  self-care for coaches 145–6
support-building
  group coaching 100–101
  Impostor Syndrome 36–8

teams, group coaching 95, 96–7
techniques *see* coaching tools and techniques
telephone coaching 73–4
testimonials, Impostor Syndrome 35
thought leaders, establishing credibility 7–9
three-way meetings 43–7
  background to the assignment 45
  coaching business 43–7
  coaching objectives 45–6
  conclusions of the meeting 46
  confidentiality 46
  contracts/contracting 43–7
  feedback 46
  success measurement 46
time boundaries 74–8
  beginnings and endings 74–5
  'door handle moments' 76
  maintaining 76–7
tools *see* coaching tools and techniques
training, Impostor Syndrome 30–3, 36–9
transformation vs change, facilitating change
    79–80

transformational learning
  facilitating change 87
  limiting beliefs 87–93
Transtheoretical Model of Change 84

'unconditional positive regard,' coaching
  relationships 128
unfinished coaching assignments, coaching
  dilemmas 111–13
unlearning, facilitating change 84–5
using this book 3

video-conferencing 73–4
voluntary work, self-care for coaches 141

walking your talk, self-care for coaches 137–9
wheel of business focus 26

* wheel of entrepreneurial traits 26–7
work between sessions, group
  coaching 100
work reviews 78
work-life balance, self-care for coaches
  137–9

zones of exploration
  assumptions zone 132
  beginnings zone 132
  coaching tools and techniques 132–5
  evidence zone 134
  familiarity zone 133
  impact zone 132–3
  maintenance zone 134
  new behaviours zone 133
  obstacles and strengths zone 133